Eric Smith

PIANOS IN PRACTICE

An owner's manual

LONDON: SCOLAR PRESS

First published 1978 by Scolar Press
39 Great Russell Street, London WC1B 3PH

Reprinted 1979

Copyright © Eric Smith 1978

ISBN 0 85967 393 6 hardback
ISBN 0 85967 394 4 paperback

Printed in Great Britain by
Whitstable Litho Ltd
Whitstable, Kent

Contents

Diagrams

Plates

excluding photographs of actions in Chapter 4

Acknowledgments

I should like to record here the help I have received from the Piano Department of Harrods Ltd, Knightsbridge, and particularly from Mr R.J. Eveleigh of that store who devoted valuable time to discussing pianos and the piano market with me. I owe a similar debt to Mr R.M. McDonagh, of Barratt & Robinson Ltd, who also provided the model upright action pictured in this book. To Mrs A. Allnutt I am grateful for the photographs, where her technical competence outshines my meagre compositional skill. Mr C.J. Smith and the Rev. S.H. Adams helped me in the provision of photographic material.

    I am much indebted also to many publications, some of which are listed at the end of this book, to owners whose pianos I have serviced and from which over the years I have gained experience which the written word cannot give, and, more personally, to Mr F.W. Allen, piano tuner, and the late Mr W. Gurney, formerly Professor at the Guildhall School of Music and Drama, both of whom unwittingly many years ago set me on this road.

    To these and many other sources I express gratitude, but they have no responsibility for the defects of this book.

Introduction

This book is concerned with the nature and working of pianos, both sick and healthy, mainly as they affect the private owner whose piano is played for pleasure.

There are at least two good reasons why an owner should be familiar with what goes on inside a piano. The first is that knowledge can help one in one's own playing. The second is that experience suggests that very many domestic pianos (if I may call them such) are inadequately maintained, even among owners who care for or celebrate the quality of their instruments. Depending on the piano (its age, its value) and the inclinations and talents of the owner, some adjustments can often be made by him personally. Alternatively, or for bigger jobs, the owner may at least be well enough informed to define exactly the symptoms in order to have the required improvements made by an expert.

So far as aiding performance is concerned, the extent of any benefit is open to dispute. I believe, however, that a knowledge of the mechanism of a piano and its adjustment makes one more critical, both with one's ears and with one's fingers. Even at the lowest level, it enables one better to define what deficiencies are one's own, what those of the instrument, and what are compounded of both. The ear comes more readily to perceive the sound lingering after it should linger. It comes to a judgment of individual and composite sounds which makes for a more discriminate use of the pedals, particularly of the sustaining pedal. It comes to a more sensitive selection of dynamic levels, to a clearer awareness of when notes are unacceptably out of tune, and it becomes more appreciative of diverse tone qualities, and so on. When these perceptions are translated into action, on the part of the pianist when playing or on the part of the tuner or technician in adjustment, the result can only be improvement, musical improvement. The fingers become more sensitive. They feel the whole progress of each key-depression. They notice irregularities of touch. They perceive subtle variations of force and timing, whether with single notes or with the components of a chord. All this goes to produce a more conscious, aware, performance.

Secondly, there is the question of maintenance. Many pianos change hands privately and are never adjusted to their best. Many purchasers are beginners, or buying for their children, or simply not very critical. A piano has so many moving parts and parts subject to compression that it is obvious that it must require, over a period, constant adjustment and attention over and above tuning, yet these it often does not receive. In due course, if neglected, the instrument will be beyond all but the most expensive and extensive restoration. Even some new pianos are bought (whether through the deficiency of the manufacturer, the retailer or his tuner) with quite obviously redundant squeaks, maladjustments and faults, and the claiming of correction under guarantee if available can exhaust even the most persistent customer. If the buyer thinks so far as to let his independent tuner look over the purchase, he has little on which to go but precedent or the recommendation of a possibly interested party when it comes to selecting such a tuner. The tuner may or may not be a good tuner and again he may, but often does not, have knowledge of regulating and adjusting a piano action and be willing to use it to practical effect. If he has the knowledge, he may not be able to find the time, and if he quotes a reasonable price for thorough tuning and overhaul he may well lose his customer.

Because pianos have stood unplayed in homes for years, because the average church, school or pub piano is in gruesome condition, all but the most critical and conscientious owners are apt to accept the fact that a piano stays recognisably in tune for many months, even years, and silently agree that, if all the notes actually 'play', money need not be spent. The piano has the great merit of stability over its antecedents like the clavichord and harpsichord but they, because they had to be tuned so much more often (and were comparatively simple to tune and adjust), received a critical attention seldom granted to the family piano.

Owners and players need to be able to ask more, and more specifically, of their tuners, and their values and consciousness need to be such that they are then prepared to pay more. Tuners and technicians need to be paid more to give of their best. Many a tuner does not, and cannot, fully tune, let alone regulate, a piano in the time which the going rate imposes on him. More of the profession are needed even with present demand. There is no simple way to raise the standards of expectation so that people would be prepared to spend more on their instruments. The piano's very virtues of completeness and stability are its weakness when compared with other instruments. The latter are played largely by enthusiasts. There is no real equivalent to the piano's occasional domestic strummer. For those who value the piano's particular qualities, however, there is much to be gained from a knowledge of its workings.

I am not suggesting in this book that owners should, one and all, 'have a go'. There are many people even in this do-it-yourself age who do not have the confidence, inclination, mechanical sense, patience and other qualities required to make them servicers of their own instruments. Moreover, a good piano is valuable, complex and delicate. Lasting and costly harm can be done by, for instance, inexpertly stabbing at hammer felts with pins; great inconvenience can be caused by misguided ventures into tuning; and uninformed or random tampering with an action can take a great deal of time to put right. I have seen tuning pins running with oil to 'prevent rust', the oil seeping into the pin-block so that the instrument can never stay in tune, and oil used in actions in order to lubricate but in time attracting dust which causes wear and a worse seizure. Tapes on an upright action are often seen to have been broken merely by careless handling of the action. Hammers on grand piano actions are broken through too casual removal of the action when the hammers are up. Pin-blocks are split by violent hammering of the tuning pins when trying to make the pins stay put. One finds actions 'regulated' so that there is no escapement and the hammers bounce on the strings, or conversely so that the keys descend without moving the hammers as much as 2mm. Hammers even on newish pianos have been softened by over-needling or by squeezing, in an effort to soften the instrument, but with the result that its tone is unspeakably dull and empty. Old hammer felts one sees filed down to the wood. Serious maladjustments of dampers, which can only have been brought about by experimental tinkering, are legion. In older instruments, nails or screws have been driven into soundboards which were loose, with the result that the boards crack. The list of catastrophes in the wake of uninformed and ham-handed 'repairs' is endless. In some ways one would rather face an instrument neglected in every way, with a view to restoration, than one which has been badly patched up.

Nonetheless, I am convinced that the greater danger is lack of information. There is stupidity as well as good sense in the mystique which sometimes seems to surround pianos and their repair. Many owners would get better professional service if they knew what might be wrong or if they could better define, in the light of improved critical faculties, what they sensed to be wrong. Moreover, I am sure that by many informed and cautious amateurs faults can be spotted before they become serious, wear can be detected while it can still be taken up by adjustment, and many defects can be corrected with little risk and great satisfaction. I know this by experience, for I have used successfully the repairs and adjustments mentioned in the last chapter of this book. The habit of playing a piano and studying its action or checking its intervals ingrains a valuation of the instrument which leads you to seek a remedy, professional or otherwise, and improves your awareness of your own playing. This must enhance the musical experience, and can help greatly if you come to that ever-difficult moment of choosing another piano. The owner who has reasonably corrected a faulty unison, or even tuned his whole piano to his own satisfaction, has not become overnight a piano tuner. Neither has the owner who eliminates a troublesome 'bounce' become a technician. Both will have achieved great satisfaction, however, and may have taken the first steps or started a rewarding hobby as well. I also believe, in no cynical way, that a more practical and informed interest of owners in their pianos would be to the advantage, not the disadvantage, of tuners and technicians. They could give better service, they would find their work more appreciated, and a more critical awareness on the part of owners would be likely to require more of them.

Anyone who has ever taken a piano action to pieces completely and correctly reassembled it will not deny that a piano is, from one point of view, a complex machine. But it is a machine with a purpose, and that purpose is ultimately mysterious; objective definitions of various tone qualities and how they are produced by the fingers striking—a mechanism which appears to leave rather little scope for producing variety of sound from variety of finger action—have yet to be found. The nature and degree of any effect which may be produced by varying the 'touch' of the fingers have always been disputed. Neither is it easy or necessarily desirable for the player to regard his piano as a machine—we speak, sometimes confusedly, of the 'touch' of a piano and of the 'touch' of a player, and we leave undefined the extent to which a particular 'tone' is due to the inherent design and materials of the instrument or to the skill of the performer in eliciting it. I have not said much of these profound matters in this book, but I hope that they will be sensed there.

One could, I imagine, work on a piano as on a car engine, or on a clock or on an electrical circuit (though doubtless the full reward for working on these things comes ultimately from seeing their lasting improvement). To me, working on a piano is working on a musical instrument of a particularly musical fascination. It may be made to have the correct measurements and to function sweetly as can be, but if it does not have a desirable touch and a variety of tonal resources the work is wasted. The crafts of wood and metal-work, intricate manual dexterity, considerable physical

3

strength, great patience and much more are involved; but it is the musical senses which set the final test and give the final satisfaction, and these senses are to a great extent individual and a matter of taste. There is no perfect piano or perfect pianist. One aims to make each instrument give the greatest satisfaction of which it is capable.

PART ONE—WHAT IS THE PIANO?

1 Distinctive qualities

The detached action

The piano is an arrangement for conveniently sounding 84–88 (or, in the smaller models, only 72) notes, which are distinctive vibrations produced by striking tensed metal wires or strings. The strings are stretched tightly across a frame in such a manner and in such proportions that the vibrations of each note are discernible as a sound pitched equally above and below its neighbours. The instrument's pre-eminent feature, enshrined in the name 'pianoforte', is that any note or combination of notes may be sounded loud or soft, according as to how the piano key is struck.

Given a certain material and diameter, a piano's string's pitch is determined by its length, in the sense of the distance between points over which it is stretched, rather than where the hammer strikes it. The latter, the 'strike point', is, however, important as partly governing tone quality, which depends on the prominence of certain harmonics or subsidiary vibrations. The string is fixed at each end and stretched over the bridge and the upper bearing bar, a heavy bar against which each string is forced, or agraffes (which are metal studs, one to each note, screwed into the frame and having the same purpose). The distance between bridge and bar or agraffe is the 'speaking length' and governs the pitch (Fig. 1). It cannot, of course, be altered save by remaking the piano.

The pitch of each string is, therefore, constant, and a string will continue to emit its pitch, when the hammer leaves it, for a time

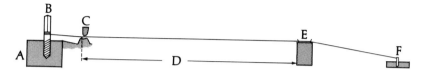

Fig. 1 Strings and speaking length
A Wrest-plank or pin-block
B Wrest- or tuning-pin
C Pressure or bearing bar pressing string onto bridge (C¹-from front or above)
D Speaking length, from bridge to pressure bar or agraffe
E Bridge
F Hitchpin in iron frame
G Agraffe holding string down onto bridge from below. (G¹-agraffe seen from front)

dependent on the length of the string and the resonance of the sounding board which amplifies its vibrations (and to which the bridge is fixed). In practice, of course, the sound is usually almost immediately deadened by pressure of a felt damper. The damper is raised automatically when a key is struck and replaced on the string when the key is released, but the dampers may also be raised independently of the keys by means of the 'loud' sustaining pedal. If this is done, the sounds of several strings coincide before dying away, and related strings which have not been struck vibrate in sympathy. The piano has no means of prolonging the sound of individual notes beyond sustaining without impediment the vibration caused by striking a string. The contact between string and hammer is momentary. Yet we know that the piano is capable of the utmost variety of sustained effect, and this apparent contradiction we shall have to consider a little further.

The clapper of a bell must leap from the bell after striking, and the drum-stick must rebound from the skin which it has set in vibration, or the inertia of the clapper or head will damp the vibration and jar as it does so. The same principle is at work in the piano which, however fluently it may sing, is a percussive instrument. If you play a note and hold the key down, the note continues to sound not because the hammer which struck the string remains in contact, but because the hammer bounces back and your key holds the damper also away; thus you can produce the same effect by depressing the right, sustaining, pedal and releasing the key— this merely means that a lever operated by your foot takes over the key operated by your finger to keep the damper off the string. In point of fact, the action is designed to throw the hammer head at the string, whence it bounces away smartly and is withdrawn by gravity in grand pianos, by a tape and spring in uprights (Fig. 2). Provided that you strike the key hard enough for the

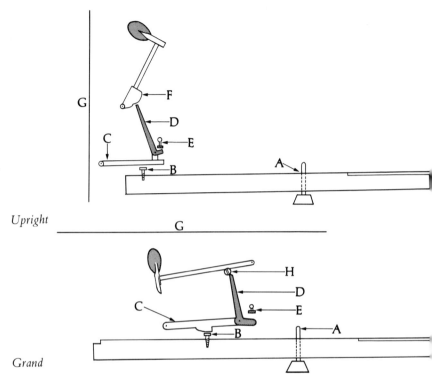

Upright

Grand

Fig. 2 Simplified diagrams of piano actions
A Key balanced on centre rail
B Capstan screw to raise wippen
C Wippen (intermediate lever) with pivoted jack attached
D Jack which impels hammer through butt or roller
E Adjustable escapement button stops jack's upward movement and disengages it from hammer before hammer strikes string
F Hammer butt
G String
H Roller, attached to hammer shank, receives jack's drive in the grand action

hammer to fly to the string, it cannot but return, with a speed initially related to that first flight, however quickly or slowly you may let the key rise (although the final part of its return is governed by how fast the key is released).

Variation of tone and volume

This detachment and its implications are certainly central to the piano and piano-playing, yet there is no general agreement on them or on the manners of playing which they may make advisable. The central importance derives from the interconnection of the force with which a hammer strikes a string, the time during which it remains in contact with the string, and the control over either which a pianist may be able to exercise. As the weight of any hammer is constant, the force means in effect the speed of impact, and that certainly is related to the speed of key-depression. That the force and the speed of actual key-depression are also related is clear from the difficulty of depressing a note fast but gently or, in practice, the very strong tendency to play more heavily as one plays faster.

Simple observation suggests that the difference between fast and slow hammer action or key depression produces a difference of volume in the sound emitted or, in terms of vibration, a difference of amplitude; hit the string harder and it will move backwards further, but will accomplish this and its return in the same time as when hit more gently, and so will produce a louder note of the same pitch or fundamental vibration (Fig. 3). Strings, however, do not vibrate only as wholes, but also in portions according to a mathematical formula, these partial vibrations giving rise to subsidiary sounds (partials, harmonics, overtones—the terminology need not bother us here) other than the fundamental pitch.

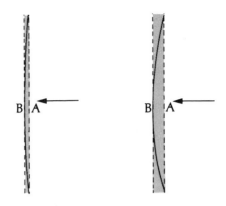

Fig. 3 Amplitude of vibration
For identical strings the time taken to vibrate between A and B is the same, the greater distance producing more volume at the same pitch

The relative volume of each of these partials varies according to the nature, tension and laying of the string and according to where it is struck, but for any string the disposition is largely constant and determines the available tone of the sound. It can be radically altered only by the tuner or technician, who may adjust the string or the hardness of the hammer felt. The hardness of this felt and the force with which it strikes the string control the duration of contact between hammer and string. The greater that duration, the more may the upper partials be damped (as, more extremely, the clapper may rest on the bell), The presence of partials, if in an acceptable series of strengths, gives 'brightness' and 'richness' to tone. If they are over-emphasised, however, or discordant partials are unduly loud, the result may be harsh and strident.

It seems that the only variation of striking which the fingers have at their command to influence the manner of striking the strings is, in the detached action, variation of velocity. We have seen briefly, however, that volume and tone are related. As to how the pianist can by his finger action subtly modify or appear to modify tone, rather independently of volume, there is no simple answer. The matter seems, however, to concern music as a sequence of and combination of notes. Generally, when we commend a pianist's variation of tone, we are not speaking of his consummate virtuosity on one note repeated devoid of rhythm. Likewise, when we consider volume, it is not, though it may be measured in decibels, a single sound against silence, but one or more sounds preceding or following other sounds. Moreover, however efficient a piano's dampers, however sparing the use of pedal and however clean the acoustic, sounds linger and merge, as do their harmonics.

Thus, although analysis can be made of partials, the mechanics of exaggerating or suppressing them, and of the particular arrangements of loud and soft partials which an audience might agree to sound 'clean', 'rich', 'thin', and so on, we can look on tone practically as the product of volume and timing variations within the inherent tonal capacity of the instrument. A passage can be made to stand out which actually is played very gently. In any chord the relative volumes of each note are variable and contribute to the tonal effect. A note can be emphasised by delay, rather than by forceful playing, and give the impression that it is louder than it actually is. Sounds can be further blended by use of the sustaining pedal. On the grand (but not on the upright, which has a different pedal system) a passage can be played loudly on two strings (for example) or softly on three, with different effect. Thus, while it

may be that the performer varies tone by varying volume, within an overall context of dynamic levels, it is volume in a subtle and relative sense and moreover closely associated with timing. If he should find that the production of a 'singing' tone, a tone surprisingly rich for its dynamic level, is furthered by a lingering caress of the keys, who are we to say that his imagination has the better of him? There is a psychology as well as a mechanism of piano touch and tonal variation, and none of these things is fully understood.

In-built factors of tone

Whatever one's skill, one cannot bring out vibrations to which the particular piano itself is unsympathetic, and a certain minimum force (dependent on the individual instrument) is required to make the hammer strike the string at all, since it does so by momentum; so that there are limits as to how gently in practice the string can be struck, just as there are limits beyond which violent striking of the string will fail to produce extra amplitude in its vibration.

Vibrancy depends on the length, weight and tension of the strings, the effectiveness of their contact with the bridge, the design of the soundboard and to some extent the case, and on associated largely fixed factors. The stringing and the pressures which it imposes at critical points are not easily or cheaply altered. Most pianos are plainly more vibrant in one register than in another—a virtual absence of tone in the short and rigid topmost strings is normal, and of course small uprights are necessarily weak in the bass (although the modern small upright has a resonance which an earlier age would scarcely credit). The modern upright can make plenty of noise, but that para-musical stage which generations of parents have called 'banging' is sooner reached than in the larger piano. The bass strings are weighted (with copper windings) very heavily to compensate for their lack of length, and therefore their sound fails to present the full harmonic series— the hammer runs into something of a brick wall.

Generally, but of course subject to quality, the bigger the piano the better, although it is accepted that the grand cannot in many homes be accommodated and that a good upright may be less constricted than the smaller grands. There are with the grand significant advantages in design and construction anyway, but it is superior primarily by virtue of its longer strings, which come nearer to varying in length and proportion to the relative frequencies of vibrations required for the true pitch of the notes and their harmonics. (Nonetheless, even the largest grand has strings fatter and shorter than the true parallel of length and frequency dictates, since the real requirement is for a string too long and too slack ever to be activated by a finger-driven hammer.) Consequently, the smaller a grand, the less great is its tonal advantage over the upright, although of course its openness of design permits a freer emission of sound. For practical purposes at home the 'boudoir' grand (some 2 metres long) is perhaps the most chosen compromise between upright and full concert (3 metres or more) grand piano.

Broadly speaking, there are three plain wire strings to each top and middle note, two lightly wound strings for each note in the tenor range, and a single more heavily wound string for each of the lowest notes. Blüthner pianos have for many years had a patented fourth string in the upper register, the extra strings being tuned to the first harmonic (an octave above) their main strings and vibrating in sympathy but unstruck. Blüthners are justly celebrated for their tone, but whether this *aliquot* stringing contributes much is debatable. Some economy models of various makes have had two strings to a note throughout the upper register. They sound rather thin and hard.

The whole subject of stringing is complex and perhaps as well approached empirically as technically. Observation indicates three highly critical issues—the point at which one changes from three strings to two strings (or from two to one) per note, the points at which gauges of wire change, and the placing, in relation to these points, of the long raised bars which normally brace the frame between banks of strings. The object of design is to secure a smooth progression of tone, without sudden change of quality, throughout. This is of course liable to be frustrated by the presence of bracing bars (omitted in some Broadwood pianos) which give a local rigidity and a gap between bridges, by the changes to thicker wire which are inevitable if the strings are to be of manageable length, and by the use of copper-wound strings in the bass to give a mass which in a single wire would be inflexible. To this end, many wire gauges are used, the gauge usually changing at about every five notes but less often in cheap models, and sometimes it is arranged that the beginning of wound strings does not coincide with a frame bar. A further object, desirable tonally and also to secure stability of tuning, is even distribution of tension throughout the frame. In this respect the massive and unnaturally short low strings, tensed more than would be a string of appropriate length and gauge, have the advantage of balancing the many highly tensioned finer strings in the treble. However, although the several changes in stringing may be perceptible, they can often be 'toned' out in some degree by softening or hardening the hammer felts around the critical points. If you are trying out a

1 **Frames and stringing** Small modern upright, overstrung

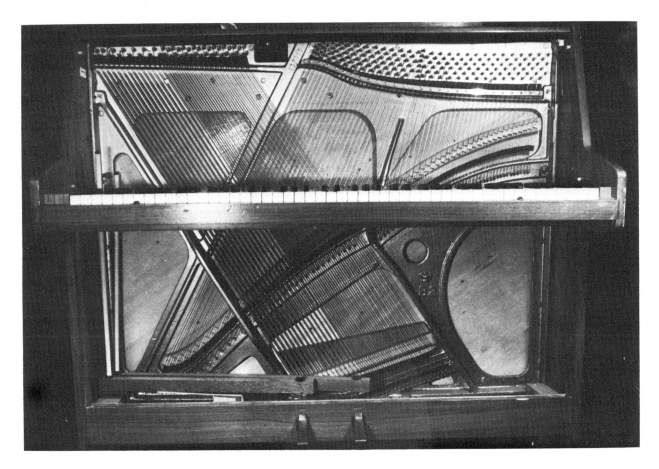

2 **Frames and stringing** Modern grand, overstrung

3 **Frames and stringing** Old larger upright, overstrung

4 **Frames and stringing** Old upright, straight strung (showing also high key capstans)

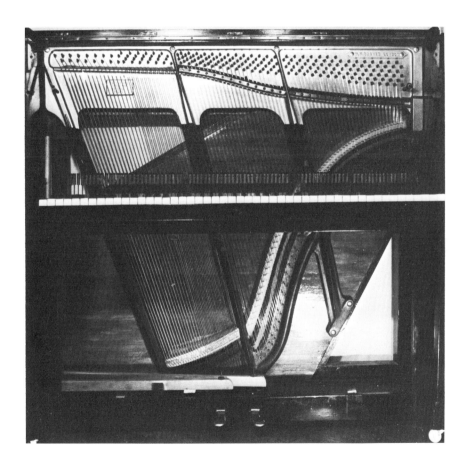

new piano it is well worth spending a moment playing short scales and chords on notes whose strings are close to frame bars, and observing whether or not tone production is acceptably even.

'Overstringing' (Fig. 4) is universal in modern pianos and is associated with these factors. 'Over-' or 'cross-stringing' is the laying of a bank of bass strings (the number of which varies but usually corresponds more or less to the number of wound strings) diagonally across the next octave or so of wire strings in the tenor range. This enables longer strings to be used than could otherwise be the case, a better spread of tension and fuller use of the amplifying soundboard area beneath the strings, and also a harmonic interaction between the one set of strings and the other, which enriches the tone. The straight (i.e. vertically) or obliquely strung piano without overstringing has in fact a certain clarity in the bass register which has some appeal, particularly in older music, but such pianos are now virtually unsaleable and the purchaser of a cheap secondhand upright piano would generally be well-advised to avoid such instruments unless he knows what he would be taking on and requires it for a special reason.

Strings pass over or under a metal bearing bar as mentioned (at the top of an upright or front of a grand). They then run across to a hardwood bridge on which are pins to limit their movement, until they reach the far end of the frame where they are anchored to or around 'hitchpins' (Fig. 1). They vibrate significantly only between bridge and bearing—otherwise they are more or less dead. The lengths of the dead portions do not very noticeably affect the sound, though sometimes they have been made proportionate to the speaking lengths just in case.

The bridge is the connection with the soundboard and both are vital to tone. In its speaking length the string must start and finish

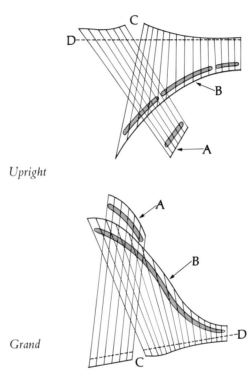

Upright

Grand

Fig. 4 General lay-out of overstringing
A Bass strings passing over main rank of strings. Bridge shaded.
B Main rank of strings. Bridge shaded.
C Location of tuning pins (top of upright, front of grand)
D Approximate line of hammers

somewhat lower than the bridge, against which it presses. In practice, strings start higher than the bridge and are forced down lower against the bearing bar or agraffes, to give them a clear starting-point. The best height of the bridge and the angle of the strings to it are known to be important in tone-production, and there are accepted bearing angles which have been arrived at empirically. The bridges—there is one long bridge, often interrupted by frame bars, and a separate raised bass bridge for the overstrings—are glued and dowelled solid with the soundboard, as to whose properties and desirable composition there has always been debate. The soundboard is the sheet of varnished wood visible behind (in an upright) and beneath (in a grand) the strings. Its purpose is to amplify, but not to modify, the small note produced by a string's vibrations, for it sets into motion a larger volume of air than the string itself can move. It presents a domed, not a flat, surface to the strings. The dome may be flattened by prolonged pressure from the strings in old instruments, and this impairs their sound for the tension in the soundboard is known to assist its vibrancy and so the tonal production of the instrument.

Factors governing touch

Such are among the relatively in-built constraints to variation of tone. Some can be modified with considerable labour and cost, but generally they are attributes of a particular instrument and the efforts of the pianist can only be directed towards making the best of what the instrument offers. Touch itself is more adjustable but, save in certain devices never brought into general use, the performer must work within the limits of the instrument as designed and as set up or regulated. Apparently heavy touch may be inherent or may be due to a certain regulation—only experience and experiment can tell. Neither a heavy nor a light touch is particularly desirable—pianists vary in their preferences—but there are widely accepted standards.

The basic requirement of the key is to drive the hammer to the string. In so doing it meets the resistance of the hammer's (and connecting levers') inertia and that of the damper with (in the upright) its damper spring. There is additionally a hammer spring in uprights to assist return of the hammer, and this resistance also is met (see illustrations in Chapter 4). The hammer moves from rest to string, a distance which is agreed to be best set at some 50mm, though the precise recommended distance varies according to make and action. This distance is influential on tone, since it affects the way in which the head strikes the string, and many old pianos will be found for various reasons to need returning to this standard. It is obvious that you do not depress a piano key this far, and it follows that leverage is involved, whereby the movement of the key (the 'key dip') at the front is some 10mm against that of the hammer (Fig. 5). This provides the necessary fast movement of the hammer but also increases the force needed to drive it from the key rather than directly, even though this is offset by the balancing of the key so that it moves more at the front than at the tail. Thus, on consideration of hammer-movement alone and leaving aside the friction in the various pivot points ('centres') of the action, the key in use is bound to present sensible resistance to the finger.

The key does not drive the hammer (via a piece known as the 'jack' or 'fly') during its full descent, for, as has been said, the last part of the hammer's journey is made by momentum with the jack detached. There is a millimetre or rather less at the end of the key's travel (before it is stopped by the felt button beneath its

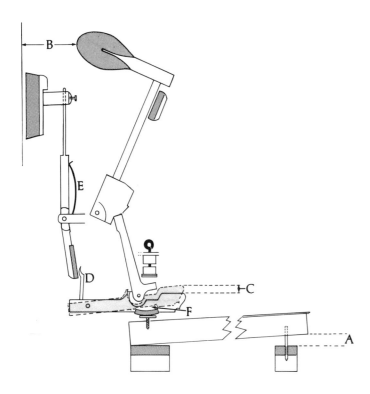

Fig. 5 Leverage and damper mechanism in upright action
A Key-dip, approximately 10mm
B Strike distance, approximately 50mm
C Wippen movement, approximately 10mm at front
D Damper spoon on back of wippen
E Damper spring, fixed to damper flange
F Movement of capstan screw, approximately 6mm

front) which is 'aftertouch', the key having done its work so far as the hammer is concerned. Keys themselves are balanced off-centre (in an upright with three parts to the front and two to the rear, for black and white keys alike), weighted so that their inclination is to tip backwards, and this is accentuated by the weight of the action parts on the key backs. This balance varies considerably. In grands, heavy hammers rest in effect directly on the keys (as is not the case in uprights), which may be weighted in such a way that they in fact tip forward when the action is re-moved. In fact, the fronts or backs of keys in pianos of any type may be weighted so as to adjust the touch in a progressive scale from heavier in the bass to lighter in the treble. (These matters are considered more fully in Chapter 4.)

The key has the other important function of raising the damper as the hammer approaches the string about to be struck, and here uprights and grands differ greatly (Figs. 5 and 6). In the grand, the dampers, visible as black wood or plastic blocks lined with felt pads over the the strings close to the hammers, fall by gravity. They are connected by individual wires to small levers in the way of the back ends of the keys, and are adjusted to be raised as the backs of the keys hit these levers on rising. They are fairly light and, as only gravity (and the small friction of centres and the felt bushes of the wires) is involved, they exert a fairly small and constant resistance to the key at all stages of its depression once they have been engaged and set in motion.

The dampers of uprights are just below the hammers (in front of the strings) and therefore known as 'underdampers', or well above the hammers and connected to the rest of the action by long wires ('overdampers'). The latter are outmoded and regarded as inefficient (since damping is at its best near the point of the

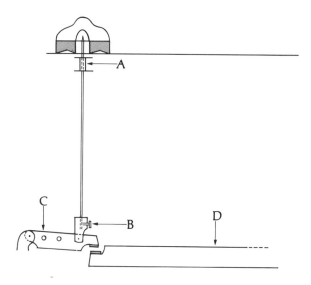

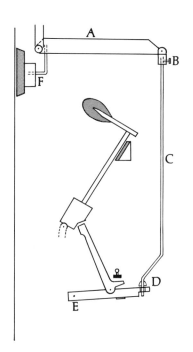

Fig. 6 Damper mechanism in grand actions
A Damper guide rail bushing
B Adjustable socket for damper wire
D Weighted damper lever
E Tail of key, which raises damper lever

hammer's impact), though they had the advantage of being easier to adjust (Fig. 7). Uprights' dampers are pressed against the strings by damper springs, the typical damper being a pivoted arm, one end engaging with the action and the other being crowned with felt varying in shape ('wedge', 'clip', 'split' or 'parallel') according to how many strings and of what type are involved. The arrangement will be clear later, but the essential points are first that the damper spring normally offers more resistance to the key than

Fig. 7 Working of overdamper upright action (obsolete)
A Sprung or weighted pivoted damper lever
B Adjustable socket for damper wire at front of action
C Damper wire
D Collar on wire and bushing on wippen where wire enters wippen at front
E Wippen
F Damper fixed by short angled wire to damper lever

5 **Piano actions** Old overdamper upright action (seen below in case
with keyboard)

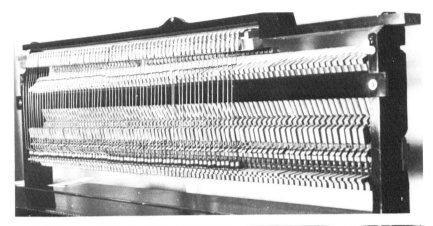

does the grand's damper, and secondly that the resistance, unlike the force of gravity in the grand, is not constant but increases as the key is depressed and the damper rises.

The point where the damper lever on a grand engages with the key is often scarcely perceptible in the touch. The point where the key's action encounters the damper spring's resistance on an upright is very much more pronounced, and the timing of this moment has to be set correctly unless the touch is to be exceedingly heavy and irregular from note to note, distracting the player from the feel of the weight of the hammer itself.

The key drives the hammer by means of the jack, a pivoted and usually sprung finger whose tip engages with the butt end of the pivoted hammer. If the key is minutely depressed on an upright the moment will be felt when the jack takes on the weight of the hammer and starts to move it. If regulation is such that the jack is engaged with the hammer from the outset, quick repetition of a note (always weak in uprights) will be impaired and in extreme cases the hammer may not fall right back onto its rest and so will not have a full striking distance (Fig. 8). There is also the likelihood that the jack will not properly engage with the hammer butt when the note is next struck. In a grand the hammer rests on a sprung lever holding it slightly above the jack's tip. This lever is raised, as is the jack, when the key is depressed, and the moment when the jack rather than the lever drives the hammer may not be perceptible. The very slight slack or 'lost motion', necessary in the upright, is apt to give the touch a less positive and direct feel than in the grand.

The main feeling of resistance in impelling the hammer occurs with 'escapement', which is readily felt as a slight 'kick' in all but the most worn actions. It occurs when the hammer is close

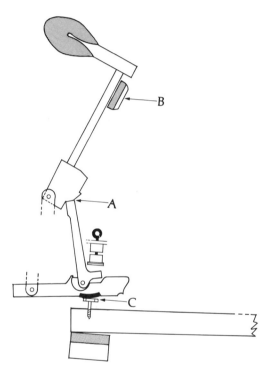

Fig. 8 Incorrect setting of key capstan
A Although the action is at rest, the weight of the hammer is resting on the jack
B The hammer shank cannot rest on the hammer rail because the jack is obstructing the butt
C The key capstan is set too high, holding wippen and jack slightly raised

to, usually some 2mm from, the string, and it is from this moment that the hammer is free of driving force and continues to the string under momentum. Escapement is brought about by arranging for an adjustable screwed felt button to intercept the heel of the jack and stop it while the wippen (on which the jack is mounted) continues to rise and the key is pressed down onto its felt pad (Fig. 2). Since the timing of escapement determines for how long the key drives the hammer, it is the most fundamental adjustment which can be made to the action, and it is a setting which does have to be altered to counter the effects of wear over the years.

It is clear that the effect of the relative timing of these resistances in the depression of a key—the weight of the hammer, raising of the damper, and escapement—must be considerable. As noted, there has to be with the upright a scarcely perceptible free movement of the key before resistance is felt. Then comes the feel of the jack engaging with and starting to move the hammer. In a grand, the weight of the hammer is effectively on from the start. The next event is the taking up of the damper, noticed in the upright as a marked and progressive stiffness, and in the grand as a slighter and completely constant increase in weight. Plainly, in either case the damper's resistance should be felt at the same stage in the descent of each key (save for those of undamped top notes). It is normally arranged to start at some 3mm of key descent, that is, when the hammer is half-way towards the string. If it occurs too early, the touch will be very sluggish and there will be a tendency of sounds to merge in fast playing. If it coincides with escapement the touch will be so heavy as to make the piano virtually unplayable and there is a chance that the string will not be completely undamped when the hammer reaches it. Escapement is set to occur as late as possible, but not so late that the head could bounce on the string because the jack did not entirely escape from the hammer butt. Clearly, early release of the hammer from the jack would represent lost power—the key would drive the hammer for a small portion of its fall and the aftertouch would be long, giving a sloppy and frustrating effect.

Nonetheless, critical as these timings are, there is room for variation and adjustment, subject to the freedom of the action's centres and the mass of its parts. Within the overall limits, the action can be regulated for players preferring a light or heavy touch or, more importantly, preferring the resistances to be felt at particular stages of key depression. Various patent systems have been used from time to time to vary touch by introducing stiffer or lighter springs with a lever, and it is often possible to alter the touch of an upright by adjusting the damper springs without seriously affecting their efficiency. Finally, of course, the poise of keys can be altered by the use of weights but, save for ironing out anomalies, this is a radical step and it is preferable not to increase the mass of the keys.

The pedals

Nothing has yet been said of the pedals, often accounted the glory of the piano. They are by no means accessories, although they can be over used. They interact most importantly with the touch both as it affects tone production and, as is not always realised, with touch as sensation. The third, central, pedal, general on American pianos and often available as an option on British and Continental pianos, has not found general acceptance in Europe and will not be discussed. It is a mechanism for sustaining individual notes whilst other notes are damped. In all but the most modern music this *sostenuto* device finds most use in sustaining a bass pedal note below various harmonies, and this effect can in fact be achieved by a quick re-depression of the right hand sustaining pedal on a two-pedal piano. Alternatively, the third pedal is a 'celeste' or 'practice' pedal, by means of which fabric is inserted between hammers and strings to produce a specially muted tone. In cheap old uprights this arrangement was often used as the 'soft' pedal.

Because of the relation of tonal richness and apparent volume, the right hand sustaining pedal is often known as the 'loud' pedal although it is of course for removing the dampers from struck (and other) strings, not for modifying the striking of the strings. In the grand, the pedal's linkage moves a wooden bar (deep in the piano below the dampers), so raising all the damper levers and the dampers (Fig. 9). Its effect on touch is fairly slight. In the upright, the pedal is linked to a cranked metal rod which raises all the dampers against their springs. The removal of the necessity to work these springs from the keys makes touch considerably lighter. This, together with unskilled difficulty in playing damped notes legato and the relatively poor sustaining power of uprights anyway, can contribute to the common tendency of players to over-use the sustaining pedal. The pedal comes to seem a short cut to faster, smoother playing, or a fuller *cantabile* tone, and the simple beauty of unison strings unconfused with their predecessors inclines to be a forgotten delight. Many a player, on becoming aware of the mingled sonorities which he habitually produces, has to go through a period of most ascetic regard to the pedal and even to ban it completely, before he can return to more discriminate and meaningful usage.

The soft pedal also readily produces unfortunate habits. Here the systems commonly used in grand and upright differ com-

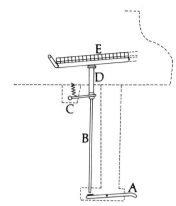

Grand
A Pedal pivoted in middle, leather pad at back end
B Pedal rod, resting on leather pad
C Sprung tongue below case body
D Dowel rod connection to inside of case
E Damper rail (shown frontways) on which damper levers rest (see Fig. 6)

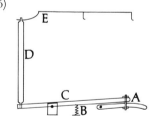

Upright
A Pedal pivoted at back, pierced by adjustable screw which holds lever. (Shown sideways)
B Pedal spring to bottom boards (C) Pedal lever
D Wooden connecting rod locates loosely in lever
E Cranked arm caused to rotate and raise damper tails resting on it (see Fig. 5)

Fig. 9 Common arrangements of sustaining pedal

6 **Piano actions** Modern upright underdamper action (seen below from rear, showing dampers)

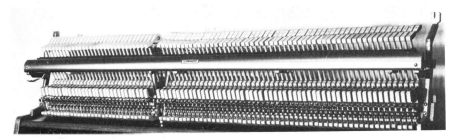

7 **Piano actions** Modern grand 'roller', 'repetition', or 'double escapement' action (note attachment to keyboard)

pletely, and so do their effects. Uprights use a 'half blow' arrangement (Fig. 10). The soft pedal connects with a movable hammer rail (where the hammers lie when at rest) and turns it forwards (that is, towards the strings) some half of the striking distance. Evidently, therefore, the hammers strike with less force for the same key-movement, and the amount of the reduction depends on how far the pedal is depressed. All this has a very noticeable effect on touch. In the first place, it greatly enlarges the slack or lost motion between jack tip and hammer butt, so that the key may be depressed nearly half of its full dip before it impels the hammer and resistance is felt. At the same time, when that resistance *is* felt, it is great, because now the starting into motion of the hammer and the raising of the damper virtually coincide. In a piano with stiff damper springs the sensation of light touch followed by meeting a heavy obstacle can be rather disagreeable, producing the paradoxical effect of playing harder to produce less sound. Not so, however, if the sustaining pedal also is used simultaneously. Then the keys have neither to raise the dampers nor to do so much work to move the hammers. At the same time the very rich sonority of raised dampers is somewhat softened, if not purified, by the soft pedal. Thus compensation may be sought in the pedals for inadequacy in the fingers and the result is that distressing habit, over-use of both pedals together. It should also be said, of course, that deliberate and discriminating use of both pedals together *is* called for in much music; one should not be misled by the popular names 'loud' and 'soft' into supposing that the pedals cancel each other out.

The grand's soft pedal works on the quite different *una corda* (or 'shift') principle. The term is historical. Nowadays *due corde*—two strings—is generally more accurate. This is a shifting of the

action (and keys) so that the hammers strike one less string (save for monochords) for each note, and plainly is an all or nothing arrangement—you strike the two strings or three, but you cannot strike two and a half (Fig. 10a). The action is rather heavy, there

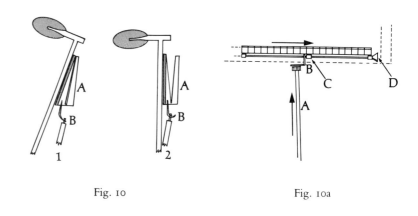

Fig. 10   Fig. 10a

Fig. 10 The 'half-blow' soft-pedal system in uprights (2-pedal depressed)
A Hinged hammer rail in two parts
B Operating lever and connecting rod from soft pedal (as Fig. 9)

Fig. 10a The 'shift' soft-pedal system in grands
A Pedal rod (see Fig. 9)
B Pivoted angled piece (design varies) working on keyframe
C Central bar of keyframe moved towards treble when pedal rod moves angled piece
D Leaf spring and stops

is no way of varying the degree of reduction, and over a long period the hammers become worn unevenly. All these factors are evidently disadvantages. So is the movement of all the keys to the right, with a certain amount of noise although as a rule surprisingly little confusion in the player.

The shift system nevertheless has two great merits, and they help to explain why attempts to introduce the 'half blow' into grands have never caught on, apart from the considerable complexity which they involve. First, the shift soft pedal introduces something which the fingers, however skilful, cannot manage, whereas the half blow arrangement is a way of regularising a lower level of force which the fingers could, after a fashion, produce alone. The reduction in the number of strings gives rise to a change in tone different from the drop in amplitude of all the strings which is brought about by the half blow system. As the hammers become worn, this difference becomes more marked and excessive, but with hammers in good order the tone becomes more lute-like, closer to that of early pianos and even of the clavichord. Secondly, the depressing of a grand's soft pedal does not produce those confusing changes in touch which we have noted in the upright. The same hammer has to be lifted through the same distance by the key, and the relative timing of this and damper movement is quite unaffected. Here again, of course, pedals can be abused, and the soft pedal may be used to mute the effects of over-employment of the sustaining pedal which, in a fair-sized grand, are more considerable. The absence of disturbance to the touch does, however, breed less in the way of bad habit. Meanwhile, the deliberate use of both pedals on a reverberant grand played softly can produce sound of extraordinary delicacy.

Such, then, are some of the attributes of the piano as they affect the pianist. At the heart is the ability to produce a particular quantity and quality (within limits) of sound at will, this by the action of the finger on a lever which impels the hammer but which is incapable of influencing the hammer at the moment of its impact with the string We have but two (or three) pedals, which add nothing to the striking of the string, compared to the multitude of an organ's stops for determining in advance different tones. The great source of strength is the variety which can be given to each separate note by a separate finger motion. Yet the scope for that is comparatively small. We cannot, as players, vary the angle at which the string is struck or the nature of the hammer head, but only the velocity of the hammer. It must remain a fascination that an instrument apparently so limited and automatic should be able to produce the subtlest exchange of tones and expressions and this, together with its large compass, its stability of tuning and its facility to play four or more parts at a time in a small room, accounts for the piano's continuing popularity.

2. Background to your piano

Predecessors

Fairly detailed histories of the piano are available and a full record is not necessary here. A knowledge of some of the forerunners and of important stages in the evolution of the piano itself does, however, conduce to more understanding of the instrument as we know it now.

The clavichord

The clavichord is most like the piano in that it, too, is a percussive instrument in which the character of each note can be varied by touch. In this respect it is supreme among keyboard instruments in that the strings are struck virtually by the keys themselves, in fact by metal projections known as 'tangents'. The clavichord is a superb instrument for intimate private playing, and there has been a great revival of interest in it from this point of view. In the privacy, however, there lies its fundamental limitation as well as its merit. It is essentially an instrument for self-expression and can hardly be used to accompany. Whilst it is true that the limitation can now be overcome by electronic means and the sound of a clavichord can be blown up to fill a hall, that for a lover of the instrument is something of a betrayal.

The cause of the limitation is precisely the direct action which, from an expressive point of view, is so exquisite. The movement of the tangent is only that of the back end of the key, in practice some 5mm (compared with the 50mm normal strike distance in a piano). There is no leverage and no intervening action to multiply this small distance (Fig. 11). If there were, expressiveness would be lost and strings would be broken, for the clavichord's strings are at very low tension and the frame is wooden. Yet, despite this great difference of scope, it was to the clavichord that the celebrators of the new pianoforte in the mid-eighteenth century looked for an example in terms of which to praise the instrument, to the clavichord whose virtue of expressiveness was to be combined with the power which had meanwhile been developed in large harpsichords.

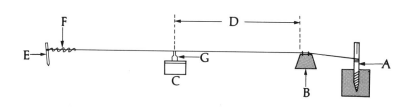

Fig. 11 Speaking length on the clavichord (cf Fig. 1)

A Tuning pin in wrestplank
B Bridge
C Key
D Speaking length when tangent strikes string
E Hitchpin
F Permanent felt damping (listing) interwoven with strings makes them dead save when met by tangent

The clavichord differs crucially from both harpsichord and piano in its registration, the means of making one note sound higher than another. As we have seen, in the piano (and in fact in the harpsichord) the speaking length is fixed for each string, being determined by the distance between the immovable bearing and the bridge. Striking the note has only the most marginal and momentary effect of altering its string-tension. In the clavichord it is quite otherwise. The pitch is determined by where the string is struck (Fig. 12). Thus in effect the tangent becomes a small removable bridge, and the string sounds only between it and the main bridge. There is then a considerable art in striking a clavichord string, and it does not come easily to the habitual pianist. If the string is not struck hard and clean, it will vibrate against the tangent and produce an unpleasant noise. If the string is struck hard and the pressure is maintained, the tension on the string will rise and the note will sound sharp. This latter effect is developed by clavichordists into a delicate vibrato regarded as essential to fine playing.

The end of the string nearest the bridge is fixed to a pin, as in the piano, which is turned for tuning. The other end runs down to a hitch-pin on the left, for the strings run from side to side across the performer. At the hitchpin end is the damping. This again is quite distinct from that of the piano. All clavichord strings are permanently damped by interwoven felt ('listing'), and if you pluck them you will find that they are more or less dead. If, however, you strike them with a firm object such as the tangent, they are of course free to vibrate between the striking point and the bridge. Thus notes are sustained and the damping is by-passed so long as the keys are held down (until the vibrations die away), but the slightest release of a key will silence its note. There is of course no equivalent of a sustaining pedal, and the damping imposes no load on the keys and touch at all.

The effective lengths of clavichord keys are all different since, whilst in practice the keys are made of the same length, the lay-out of the strings from side to side demands that the tangents for the highest note will be at one corner and that for the lowest note will be diagonally opposite at the other corner (Fig. 13). The snag with this arrangement, which from the point of view of furnishing is obviously convenient, is that the diagonal line of the tangents

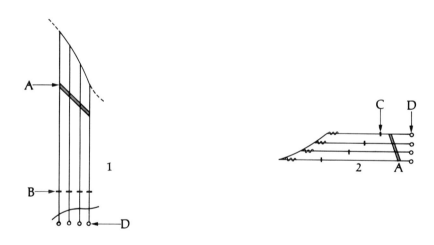

Fig. 12 Registration: 1) harpsichord/piano (grand); 2) clavichord
A Bridge
B Strike point of hammers or plectra
C Strike point of tangents
D Tuning pins

limits the area of soundboard which can be used, since clearly it must not impede the tangents. Thus the soundboards of instruments—clavichords, virginals, square pianos—with this layout are mainly to the right-hand end. The small soundboards, wooden frames and relatively slack strings are, with the direct action, the explanation of the intimate character of the clavichord.

A clavichord's touch is exceedingly light. There is nothing for the player to feel other than the inertia of the key itself (which is balanced lightly backwards) and the impact of tangent and string, which remain together for precisely as long as he chooses. The most minute gradations of tone and volume can be produced for any note and the effect of varied touch can be anticipated precisely. It is a delightful instrument, pre-eminent in its narrow field which has much in common with that of the piano. Yet it is very different from the piano, and it is not easy to move from playing the one instrument to the other.

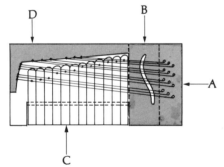

Fig. 13 Simplified diagram of clavichord lay-out
A Wrestplank, tuning pins and soundboard (shaded) beneath
B Bridge
C Keys, with tangents on tails beneath strings
D Wooden frame with hitchpins

The harpsichord family

The harpsichord arises from dissatisfaction with the limitations of the clavichord, particularly as to sonority and power. It is an instrument capable of solo performance for public pleasure and of accompaniment, and can play its part in a concerted work (as opposed to a piano concerto in which the piano may enter into dialogue with full orchestra or be heard above it). There are several members of this group of instruments, principally the virginals, spinet and harpsichord. Distinctions between them are not always made clearly and we shall not distinguish them beyond the convenient formula that virginals have strings at $90°$ to the keyboard (as in the clavichord), the spinet appears more like a grand piano somewhat askew (the strings running at some $45°$ to the keyboard), and the full harpsichord is laid out much as a grand piano, with strings in the same direction as the keys (Fig. 12). There is no form corresponding to the upright piano with strings vertical or nearly so.

The harpsichord differs radically from clavichord and piano in that it is a plucked instrument, not a percussive one. It flourished from the sixteenth to eighteenth centuries, considerably co-existing with the older clavichord, which it did not show signs of superseding until itself all but superseded fairly suddenly at the end of the eighteenth century. Direct plucking will produce more volume than direct striking by tangent; the strings were of increasingly higher tension and, for all except the virginals, a larger soundboard was permitted by the layout. There can hardly be any doubt that the harpsichord's popularity was due to its capacity as a performing instrument, rather than purely as a means of self-expression for the player. At the same time, it did not have, as early promoters of the piano remarked, the expressiveness, the facility for making an individual note loud or soft, characteristic of the clavichord and of the piano.

Plucking is performed by an upright piece, the 'jack', at the end of the key (Fig. 14). The jack has a hinged tongue with a plucker or plectrum of quill (though synthetic materials are used in modern instruments) mounted on it so as to stick out beneath the string. The tongue will not permit the plectrum to move out of the path of the string as the key back rises, and so the plectrum forces its way past the string, causing it to vibrate. As the key returns, the tongue is so hinged and sprung that the plectrum is almost noiselessly pushed aside, returning ready for action once it is free of the string. Damping is more akin to that of the piano than to that of the clavichord in that each key has an individual damper, being a slip of felt so placed as to rest on the string when the key back and jack are down. On the other hand, compared with the piano damper, the harpsichord damper imposes no increased resistance to touch, being in effect part of the mass of the key.

The pitch of harpsichord strings is determined not by where they are struck, but, as in the piano, by their speaking length between bridge and bearing. Consequently, the plectra can be laid out in a straight line and the soundboard can cover a large area of the strings. In the eighteenth century harpsichords became progressively more massive and many stops and elaborations were introduced, partly to compensate for the inflexible nature of the instrument's tone. Volume was increased partly by design, tension of the strings and so on, and partly by the adjustment before performance of the depth of engagement between plectra and strings. This depth has of course considerable influence on the feel of the touch.

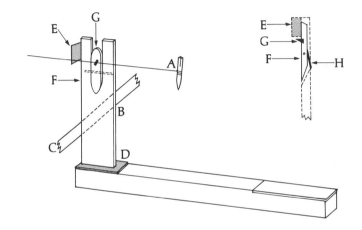

Fig. 14 Principle of harpsichord family actions
A String and tuning pin
B Body of jack
C Wooden jack guide
D Base of jack rests on key tail
E Damper moves up and down with jack to which it is fixed
F Wooden tongue pivoted in middle of jack on pin. Can only turn one
   way (see detail)
G Plectrum driven into tongue
H Bristle spring returns tongue to vertical after it has been brushed aside
   by string on the jack's descent

However a harpsichord is 'voiced'—that is, however the plectra are adjusted—the distinctive kick of the plucking, as felt in the touch, is lighter than the corresponding sensation in a piano's escapement, and there is a more noticeable aftertouch as the key moves down to the felt on the key-bed—for of course the plectrum must come clear above the string. The key dip is in the region of 8mm and of this the act of plucking takes up slightly less than half. It is clear from these small figures that it is not possible very substantially to vary plucking or, therefore, tone or volume for individual notes. As with the piano action, so with the harpsichord an initial force is required to accomplish the object at all. If the plectrum is set short or shallow, then this force will be slight, and if it is set deep the force will be larger, but the initial requirement is determined when the instrument is set up, not by the player's playing.

There is no magnification by leverage comparable with that in a piano action, and fast or slow movements of the keys, provided they exceed the necessary minimum, can have little effect on the plucking or the sound produced. With a skilled performer, they may have some. Nonetheless, the main variation and expressiveness of harpsichord music must be found in subtlety of rhythm and in the enriching and sustaining of tones by trills and ornaments.

Points in the evolution of the piano

Types of piano

The earliest pianos were what we should now call 'grand', being of the harpsichord 'wing' (*flügel*—the German for grand piano) shape, with strings horizontal and running forward from the player in line with the keys. Essentially domestic pianos were made from about 1770 onwards as square pianos. These took their form from the clavichord and virginals, the strings being at right-angles to the keyboards and the soundboards being relatively small. Simple actions were used with very light hammers, the heads, which were often almost globular in shape, pointing away from the performer. The firm of Broadwood pioneered the placing of the wrest-plank (pin-block) along the back of the instrument, rather than to the right-hand side as in clavichords, and this fashion was very soon adopted at the start of the nineteenth century. Damping was on the same principle as in the modern grand, but of course lighter. The strings were at low tension and neither the light touch nor the quality of the sound produced by these early square pianos much resembles what we should consider as pianistic. In England, however, Broadwood (the leaders) and others produced them in great quantities until about 1840. In the United States, volume production continued until the end of the century, when cast iron frames and high-tension stringing were used. The 180° lay-out of the strings entailed, however, a soundboard small in relation to the area covered by the strings and was probably a contributory reason for the square piano's decline. The later square piano was moreover a very massive piece of furniture which by its nature could only be relieved by decoration. The upright, when developed, was inherently more comely, bizarre as some of the older uprights may now seem. (It should be noted that the term 'spinet' was, and often still is, mistakenly applied to the square piano rather than to the true plucked instrument of that name. 'Spinet' is also now used to indicate the virtually topless mini-upright, with an action dropped below the keyboard-level, which is made on a small scale in England but very widely in the United States.)

The upright 'vertical' as opposed to the 'horizontal' grand and square piano) was invented towards the end of the eighteenth century. Early forms, such as those known as 'giraffe', 'cabinet' and 'upright grand', turned the grand's lay-out through 90° and made little use of the space between the keyboard and the floor. Subsequently, stringing was taken to the bottom of the instrument and also sloped obliquely to reduce overall height. What really held up development of the upright, however, was the absence of an efficient action in which springing could play the part played by gravity in a grand together, perhaps, with the presence of a taste for the ornate and monumental when the limited floorspace required of an upright would now seem to lead logically to an instrument smaller in all dimensions. In fact, the invention of a suitable action (discussed below) coincided with a movement to simpler and smaller instruments. The upright, having reached this stage, rapidly took over the market formerly (in England) existing for square pianos, although for a short while in the middle of the nineteenth century France led the way in producing upright pianos.

In considering the merits nowadays of the three main types of piano (the square, the grand and the upright), the square can be ruled out save as an antique or near-antique which has its pleasures of a special sort if well-restored. It cannot offer what the modern ear regards as acceptable piano-tone or the modern finger accepts as piano-touch. Between the grand and upright the choice may be more difficult, however, although it is usually a question of how much priority can be given to musical values, if the budget will stretch.

Let it be said clearly that there can be no doubt whatever that the grand piano is superior in principle to the upright, mechanically and musically. If you have plenty of room, this is partly a matter of size; a grand piano of nine feet long is acceptable, indeed magnificent, when an upright on the same scale is simply impracticable and not made. The grand *tends* to have longer strings, and this is an enormous advantage. If you buy a mini-grand, you may settle for strings barely longer than in a good-sized upright, and that can be a difficult decision for the grand will cost considerably more and may be of less good quality. But all grands, of whatever size, have other inherent advantages. Many players prefer their soft pedal action, but opinions differ on this. There is no denying, however, that the use of gravitational force rather than springs in the action is a benefit, as is the largely open area of strings and soundboard which grands, even with their lids down, present. Their touch, though it may appear heavier, is more consistent and revealing, their damping is more reliable and less prone to wear (though more prone to vary from changes in climate). Their construction involves the bonding of the soundboard and a specially constructed rim to the case, which makes the instrument very much more resonant and able to sustain vibration longer. Most grand actions, whilst more complex to regulate, can be regulated more exactly, and they offer better repetition of notes (a point to which we shall return). Finally, although of course there have been and are grands for the cheaper market, a grand will always be more expensive than its upright equivalent, finished and adjusted as it is with more thoroughness. It is a false generalisation that grands are made for and used by musicians, whereas uprights are for families, students and church halls, but there is an element of truth in it nonetheless.

What, then, can one say of the aspersed upright? First, there is an enormous range of upright pianos new and second-hand. Some were mass-produced (to the extent that any piano even now is mass-produced, for there remains, at least in England, much of craft in the industry) to as low a price as possible; others were made to produce a decent compromise between musical values and what could be accommodated in a living-room; and still others attempt to do all that can be done, whether musically or in finish and materials, to represent musical instruments of the highest value, and will indeed cost more than the cheaper grands, particularly those from abroad. Secondly, whilst the essence of the upright is compromise, it is compromise such as has for over a century commended itself for domestic music-making, an activity which would have suffered very greatly if there had been no alternative to the grand.

Since the second world war the alternatives of clavichord, virginals and spinet have been accepted by many amateur musicians for older music. This is admirable, though it is not to say that such music cannot be played also on the piano. A very great deal of the classical repertoire was, however, written specifically for the piano and can hardly be played on anything else, however different may be the modern piano from that of a hundred and fifty years ago. The roundness of piano tone, the highly tensioned strings and the felt hammers, as also the effects of the pedals, can be quite acceptably captured in a good upright piano, and there is no reason to feel that with an upright you are not getting the real thing, though certainly you are getting a limited version.

The action

More will be said of modern actions in Chapter 4. For the moment we are concerned with significant points in their evolution. Many of the basic principles were first gathered into practice by an Italian harpsichord-maker, Bartolomeo Cristofori, from 1709 onwards. He seems clearly to have decided that variation of dynamic for each note was required, and that it would have to be produced by percussive rather than plucking action. To this end, he used a light hammer, arranged with the head pointing away from the performer and striking the string from below, as in the modern grand. He activated this hammer by a sprung upright jack, mounted on the key itself but driving an intermediate pivoted lever, retained as the 'wippen' of later actions. The whole arrangement created leverage, by which a large movement of the hammer corresponded to a small movement of the key, and also a simple escapement, for the key and the hammer were separate and detached as the tangent and key of the clavichord were not. At the same time, he had a damper falling onto the string and raised by the tip of the key when a note was played. Subsequently he also arranged for a 'check' to catch the hammer on its falling away with the key hold down, and so to prevent it from bouncing back onto the string. His action could be shifted by a hand operated stop, to play on one string rather than two strings, the principle continued in grands till this day.

The other historic development of seminal importance for the grand action was that of the French Sebastien Erard, whose so-called 'double escapement' action of 1822 is now in principle employed in all grand pianos, although there were other simpler actions in use throughout the nineteenth century and indeed occasionally later. It is the double element—not in strict fact a double *escapement*—that characterises Erard's contribution and has been adopted generally. For the moment it will suffice to say that the double action has not only the usual intermediate lever (the wippen) with the jack pivoted to it, but also a sprung lever pivoted at the other end of the wippen. The function of this second lever is to cushion the fall of the (increasingly heavy) hammer, and to raise it up by the spring's tension after a blow in which the key is partly but not fully released. The hammer is then high enough for the jack to return beneath it and to deliver a further blow. Thus when the hammer is released from the check it does, after all, bounce back, but in a delayed fashion and (if adjustment is correct) not far enough to hit the string unless the key is again depressed. By this means the time between a note and its repetition can be greatly reduced, for the hammer has not to return fully to rest, nor the key to be entirely released, before the note can be sounded again. This has a notable effect on the playing of trills, turns and indeed all rapid, especially quiet, passages as well as in the repetition of a single note.

As has been said, early attempts to make an upright piano (that is, with the strings and hammer shanks nearly vertical) brought the idea into disfavour because the actions were unreliable and slow in performance. The real development of the upright stems from the invention by a Londoner, Robert Wornum, of a tape-check action, whose principle spread rapidly over Europe after its introduction in 1826. Early actions did not, despite the development of the grand, employ effective checks to the hammers. Consequently, repetition had to be delayed until the key and hammer were completely returned and the jack or driving device could come into position for another blow, and, in addition, hammers were liable to bounce. A check situated on the wippen, such as Wornum employed, caught the hammer and allowed the jack to snap back into place. Wornum also accelerated the return of the hammer by the now familiar tapes. The great merit of these is that they impose no resistance to the touch (or to the hammer's advance) but tauten for that period after striking when the key has moved in advance of the hammer, thus jerking the hammer back into a swift return. A mild hammer spring was, and is, used in addition, and the part played by the tape varies. It has the further function of keeping the otherwise separate hammer and wippen (jack) units linked, but not in such a way that the detachment of the action is lessened. This will be clear from the illustrations in Chapter 4.

Wornum's and previous upright actions had their dampers placed well above the striking point of the hammer, with an adjustable linkage to the wippen or other moving part, the over-damper system already mentioned (see Fig. 7). In the horizontal piano the damper was from the first placed much nearer to the striking point where, as we have seen, it is more effective. This doubtless arose because of the simplicity of operating the damper by contact with the end of the key, which is not practicable in the upright. No single date can be assigned to the introduction of what is now the universal underdamper sprung arrangement for uprights. Underdampers seem to have become general from the beginning of the twentieth century. On grands the modern arrangement is seen in the earliest forms, though there have also been systems with the dampers coming up from below the strings, as, rather oddly, of hammers striking strings from above.

Strings and frames
If we can see the piano as in part a return to the expressiveness of the clavichord, we can see it also as part of a long evolution from the quiet to the possible loud, which corresponds in part to the

growth of public performance on a wide scale and the fostering of the virtuoso. In this evolution heavier hammers, heavier and stronger strings, together with tougher and more stable frames, are interconnected.

In general, early keyboard instruments were strung with steel or brass. Wound (also known as 'covered' and 'spun') strings for greater mass and lesser length, yet with greater flexibility than that of the corresponding gauge of solid wire, were introduced at the end of the eighteenth century. Short treble strings were doubled or trebled at an early stage, with the object of increasing their vibrancy. Cristofori's pianos had two strings throughout and this was common in clavichords. Modern practice is to use one string in the bass, two strings in the tenor and three higher up but (as has been said) the number of notes in each register varies according to design. So far as the piano is concerned, over-stringing was introduced by Henri Pape in about 1840, and it was rapidly adopted in high quality pianos. Plain-strung pianos, however, lingered till well beyond the end of the century, and in the case of uprights plain-stringing and over-dampers are most often found together.

The trichords of modern pianos are for the most part made of wire bent at the hitchpin and sent back to the next tuning pin (Fig. 15). In consequence, each side of an alternate pair of wires is at a different pitch from the other, though in practice the tension and friction at the hitchpins seem to ensure that there is little difficulty in tuning these conjunct strings to their individual pitches. The arrangement was patented in 1827, but the earlier practice (of a single wire, eyed at the hitchpin, for each string) continued in some degree throughout the nineteenth century and survives in some modern pianos of high quality, for example

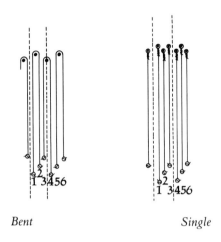

Bent   *Single*

Fig. 15 Bent and single stringing of trichords
Strings 1–3 are tuned to one pitch and strings 4–6 to the next semitone

by Blüthner and Bösendorfer. Bechstein and other makers of proverbial repute also use agraffes over the whole range, including the extreme treble where the cheaper and stronger bearing bar is more general (Fig. 1).

In the last half of the nineteenth century improved processes made steel wire of much greater tensile strength available for piano strings. This went hand in hand with the furtherance of cast iron frames, since they alone (with the exception of steel, which has been used) had the necessary rigidity and stability for extremes of climate. The date of the first complete iron frame cannot be given since there are difficulties of definition. Prototypes were made earlier, and they were many systems of bracing bars, but a complete iron frame was still a novelty in 1850 and was not generally adopted until towards the end of the century. Nowadays, where our heating systems can produce extremes of temperature and aridity almost greater than those that exist in the raw climate, one would be most unwise to contemplate buying a wooden-framed piano unless for some particular historical reason or unless special arrangements could be made for its care. Moreover, specialist consultation is needed to establish a safe pitch to which such an instrument may be tuned.

There is, however, a deterrent other than fragility and that is the different sound produced by strings of relatively low tension and the lighter hammers associated with them. The silvery sound of an old piano, for example of a good grand with bracings dating from about 1850, is not what we, having evolved through the ages of Liszt and Rachmaninov and being well aware by record-ings or actual experience of the timbres of clavichord and harpsi-chord, would expect of a piano. Even if it were of acceptable appearance and in good order, you could not buy such an instru-ment and persuade the children that it was just the same as, or better than, the piano at school.

The hammers

The hammers, being apparently so simple and so much the pro-ducts of a craft industry, have a claim to being the most intriguing part of the piano; and indeed, with the strings, they have the most essential part to play in the quality of sound which it generates. Even now, composition varies from make to make, and the best material with which to strike the string has over the centuries been one of the most frequent objects of experiment.

The ear seems to demand that a slack string be hit (or plucked) by a hard substance and a highly tensed string be struck by a relatively soft substance. Some of this is due to the effect of the contact of string and hammer which has already been noted. A compromise has to be found between lingering on the string and damping out the partials which produce life and brightness, and darting to and from the string so that the impression is of hardness and thinness with a less clear fundamental pitch. Even on the harpsichord this dilemma arose, and countless materials have been tried (and continue to be tried) for the plectra in search of a good compromise tone or for special effects; for the piano, with great possible variation in the force of striking, the problem is even greater. When leather plectra enjoyed a vogue in the late eighteenth century claims for them were such as almost to suggest that a new instrument had been invented.

Such, however, was virtually the case with Henri Pape's intro-duction of felt for a piano hammer in 1826. Hitherto, the most usual covering had been a soft leather, usually buckskin, sometimes in layers with wool and cotton. Hammers by modern standards were light in weight and shallow in depth. In the early square pianos they resembled small leather-capped balls rather than the wooden splints with felt on either side with which we are familiar.

As more massive strings were tensed more highly, they could be vibrated only by heavier hammers. The problem then was to obtain a relatively soft yet durable outside to cater for soft playing, and a really firm base which would stir the whole string, moreover to graduate from the soft to the hard and to ensure that the hammer would not be cut to pieces in a short time. The great benefit conferred by felt was its combined tension and compression when bent and pressed round a wooden mould. Nevertheless, it was until recently still common to tip old treble hammers with buckskin where the felt had worn through—and this is still a more satisfactory expedient in an emergency than to patch up with soft, untensed felt.

Modern hammers are formed from a single wooden mould for all 72–88, onto which tapered felt is pressed and stuck by machine, before the sections which will be individual hammers are cut out. Great improvements in consistency and tapered pressing of the felt have been made, so that the thickness, tension and weight are carefully graded for the scale. The work of 'toning' is broadly to adjust the surface tension and inner compaction to produce even tone whether the piano is played loud or soft. It is carried out at length on a new piano in the factory, and becomes necessary from time to time thereafter according to wear and taste.

Modern pianos

Although there have been changes in appearance and in production methods, the instruments made today do not differ essentially from those made seventy years ago or more. The fundamentals of actions, bridges, soundboards, and so on, remain the same. The most substantial changes have been in the direction of making universal some improvements which for a long time seemed to hold fire (underdamping and overstringing of uprights, for example). Many radical innovations, particularly to the keyboard, have been suggested but not taken into mass-production. Some notable changes made for special purposes (such as the placing of the action below and sometimes behind, in small uprights) have not affected the design or even greatly the proportions of the majority of instruments. So long as the tone of the wire struck by

felt continues to be preferred, this continuity will persist, for there is no way round the constraint of a practical minimum length of string, and there is general agreement as to what that length is. For the moment, the great popularity of concerts of classical music based on a somewhat small repertoire gives one no reason to think that the conventional piano will before long be replaced by a similarly universal keyboard instrument producing sound of a different character.

Nevertheless, the post-second world war upright is fairly distinct in appearance, and particularly so by its smallness, even excluding the 'minis' which have very little casing above keyboard level. The old upright 'parlour piano' was not as a rule less than 120cms high or 30cms deep from back to front—and this depth continued to the top. Modern uprights which strike us as deliberately compact may be around 98cms high, the standard medium-priced models tend to be around 110cms, and even the larger and more powerful uprights are seldom more than about 115cms high. Depth measured just above the keyboard may still be in the region of 30cms, but modern cases almost invariably taper to a top much narrower, say around 12cms.

Such changes, though numerically they appear slight, greatly affect appearance and of course they are possible partly because of alterations within. Actions have dropped and even turned through 90° so that the capstan meets the wippen foot on its side and the jack is nearly horizontal. The old abstracts (linking keys and wippens) and high capstans have gone, the strings have been shortened and the angle of overstringing increased with a consequence that low pianos tend to be on the long side. There are degrees in all this, and it will be noticed that the most expensive pianos are not the smallest, nor do the most celebrated makes of the past turn out the instruments which are most modern or convenient in proportions. It may be guessed that the really small upright appeals to the lower end of the domestic market where perhaps music is to be accommodated rather than to rule the house. This trend has gone even further in the United States with its popular 'spinet' model. Despite their limitations, however, the more compact models look like being a sound investment and would hardly be bought without some musical interest, for there is a dearth on the secondhand market and a new piano of any description involves a considerable capital outlay. Where the piano is to be discreet in sound and appearance, or where available space leaves no choice, the typical small modern upright has obvious merits and it goes into households where previously a piano might hardly have had access.

The grand has not undergone comparable changes. Grands down to 165cms or less in length were made early in this century and the 140cms grand seems (to judge by current secondhand sales) to have been particularly popular in the rather lean inter-war period. These lengths include the keyboard, and such grands have strings almost as short as those of uprights. The grand must occupy more floor space then the upright, and neither musically nor physically can it be much further reduced—though, so far as appearance goes, the open space beneath a grand lessens the heaviness which its overall size would otherwise suggest. As has been noted, the grand has distinct advantages in the action over the upright, but these advantages will not inevitably commend the smallest grand over a good medium or large upright.

The appearance of all pianos, but of uprights particularly, has tended towards greater lightness both of contour and indeed of colour, since lighter woods with visible grain have come into vogue in furniture generally. Not only are the tops of uprights tapered back (dispensing with back beam structure and using a fuller metal frame), but the columns and extended toe-blocks beneath the keyboards of a former age have gone with the candlesticks; if, indeed, they have not gone, they can be removed according to taste from an older piano and the castors be set back, for the columns are not essential to support or balance. Ornament, save in reproduction pieces where it sometimes seems overdone, is rare, and makers' names are plain and discreet in lettering. On grands, plain or fluted supports have generally replaced the old lyre pedal trapwork (and on many makes did so early in this century), but this is often still available as an optional reproduction style. Uprights' music rests are ledges hinged to the inside of the fall, or the edge of the fall itself. They are often less efficient than the old hanging rests and hold music books too near to the vertical. They have, however, the advantage that making the piano ready to play with music does not involve an intricate tussle with the hanging type of rest. Music clips are rarely fitted, being replaced by a slight ledge or by rubber-headed nails; this often seems a misjudgement by manufacturers, but good clips are not hard to make from brass wire tapped at the ends with a thread. Many smaller uprights have props for the lid to be raised, as in a grand and as if in acknowledgement of small tonal output. On grands it is usual to provide both a short and a long prop for the main lid. The 'rose' catch for the main lid has, with a few exceptions, gone, and reading rests are usually a sheet of shaped wood rather than intricately scrolled fretwork.

A great deal of case-work is now made of compressed wood fibre with veneer, partly because hardwood is in short supply and costly, and many former foreign sources are not available. The cultured impulse is to prefer solid wood but, in being less subject to warping under modern dry heating conditions, the 'manufactured' wood may well be superior, and at least it cannot be released onto the market inadequately seasoned. The same climatic advantage attends the cold glues now used in making laminated wrestplanks, bridges and the rims of grands. (Heated animal glues are still used, however, for certain jobs, particularly in the action, where a joint may at some future date have to be loosened.) Nylon and plastic are increasingly used in centres, jacks, flanges, key bushings and even wrestpin bushings. They are thought to be more durable, and the mass-produced article is more easily fitted, than the traditional materials at such points. Actions generally are produced by specialist firms (for example, Herrberger Brooks, British Piano Actions, Renner), but there are exceptions, such as the firms of Blüthner, Steinway, Knight, Bentley, and Barratt and Robinson. Save that the firms are less numerous, this situation of outside specialist parts manufacturers differs little from that of seventy years ago. Casting frames is almost entirely the work of specialist foundries and always has been, although a few manufacturers own their foundries which are used for other contract work.

The once highly-prized french polish finishing of pianos is now seldom carried out, save by restorers in a small way of business. When french polishing is used—and, though not very hard-wearing, it has a unique lustre—it is usually rubbed down to a satin finish. The preference is rather for oiled or sealed finishes which show the grain, and give some suggestion of the natural colour of the veneer, for which teak and mahogany are most popular. A high-gloss sprayed polyester finish is used also, more plastic-looking in black than an ebonised and french polished surface, but applied more quickly and being tougher.

Buying a piano

This is not a sales manual and is not the place for personal opinions and preferences with regard to various names of piano. Buying a piano, assessing one's own or someone else's piano, or, at worst, being asked to assist in the purchase of a piano—these are, however, all natural consequences of a practical interest in the subject, so that a few remarks are appropriate. The diffidence comes from a realisation that choosing or evaluating an instrument is an individual and subjective matter, and if two people can agree that they prefer the same piano out of a group it remains unlikely that they can give a really convincing and reasoned justification of their preference.

Modern pianos are of a very high average quality ; really defective or even short-lived pianos are not made. The basic cost of any piano is so considerable that the cutting of a few corners for the sake of a slightly lower price is hardly worthwhile. Various makes of new piano may be preferred for different reasons in the confidence that anyway you have a reliable and musical instrument. Old pianos vary so much according to treatment, simple age of the design, and restoration that remarks on the characteristics of a particular make may well mislead. Though one has come across such descriptions, it may be neither helpful nor accurate to refer to the 'mellow Bechstein', 'the refined Bösendorfer', or 'the bright Steinway'—or, on the cheaper new front, to 'the discreet Welmar', 'powerful Danemann', 'small but precise Zender', and so forth. All these and similar ones are relative terms, and what they relate to is unclear. Yet the factual information in manufacturers' hand-outs is often meagre and indeed would generally not be understood if it were any more detailed. Moreover, there are few mechanical differences of detail which are not the subject of disagreement among retailers (who may not be disinterested), tuners and pianists, and none which could lead one reasonably to give blanket condemnation of one maker's pianos over another. New pianos, high as is their average quality, do cover a wide price-range, and the reasons for their doing so are many, though certainly quality of workmanship and materials is one of the more general ones. How *can* one personally arrive at the best value for money and the instrument most satisfactory over future years, save by luck?

In the end, the intending purchaser or the owner taking stock of his piano can only make his own decision by extensive comparison of sound and touch. If he relies on the advice of others, as of course he sometimes must, he may well find himself disappointed, for it is very hard to understand, let alone to translate into words, another's requirements here. One should be particularly careful not to pay undue deference to names, especially where it is a case of secondhand versus new. The classical names—perhaps I can chance Bösendorfer, Blüthner, Steinway, Bechstein and Grotrian-Steinweg in particular but in no order—are not classical names without good reason, and they are not names merely from the past. Their pianos are still among the most expensive and still among the best investments, not only for musical reasons. One has, however, to consider that these are reputations founded on the advertisement of the greatest artists of the piano primarily, and only secondarily of their humble imitators and followers. They relate primarily to concert grands (though this is not to belittle smaller instruments from the same and comparable houses), and most domestic owners cannot accommodate a concert grand or, indeed, afford to buy one new from any such maker. Even a thoroughly reconditioned grand of smaller size

and perhaps seventy years old may be magnificent or deeply unsatisfactory for many reasons. You take a very big risk in buying secondhand in the 'name' market, though certainly the gains may be correspondingly large. The modern upright is far more flexible and resonant, even if smaller, than many an upright of famous make a century old. Moreover, it is likely to be better suited to modern living conditions and to require less maintenance over the years.

The modern English upright range, by such as Chappell, Knight, Broadwood, Kemble, Barratt and Robinson, Zender (firms old and new, in no special order and omission implies no slur) is virtually a new generation of upright piano going into our houses in great numbers, suitable for family practice but not to be spurned by advanced musicians, and attractive as furniture. The range of English grands is somewhat smaller, Welmar (Whelpdale, Maxwell and Codd) and Challen (Barratt and Robinson) being among the leaders here and, in view of the larger sums at stake, it is as well to look also at new and secondhand models of famed (and other) foreign names. The relative price of English pianos changes considerably according to ruling exchange rates. East German pianos are in effect subsidised and very competitive in price and quality. The Japanese and Russian models now widely available are competitive in price, finish and quality. They do, however, as yet seem to lack distinctive character, both in tone and appearance, though the Japanese tend, with the Americans, to prefer a tone bright compared with that favoured by those German manufacturers who founded their reputation in the last century. The public is indeed being educated, at least in England, to a bright tone by the wide use of Steinway pianos in concert and on the media, and even Bösendorfer, known for its quiet purity, now seems to be producing models with a sharper tone.

Subjective as the choice must be, if you can avail yourself of apparently impartial technical advice, perhaps from a tuner, you should do so. It is not easy in a few moments to distinguish incorrigible from temporary defects and faulty regulation in the action, or poor tuning from faults in the resonant side of the piano which will, at best, be costly to correct. Take as much time as you can and do not be diffident in playing whatever you like. The salesman is not there to give you marks for your playing and, if he compliments your musicianship or good taste and advises a more expensive instrument, be wary. It is often said that a piano is a good investment financially. So, in certain terms, it has proved to be, but it is not necessarily an investment easy to realise with a view to correcting an error in judgment. The dealer, even in part-exchange, expects to make a considerable mark-up on any piano which you trade in, for restoration is expensive and pianos are slow stock often sold new, though shop-soiled by a few months, below current prices. Here, of course, bargains are to be had. Selling privately does, of course, tend to give a better return, but remember that many of the prices asked are never reached and many private advertisers end up by selling for less to the trade. Buying privately is fraught with great risks, particularly, of course, in the case of older instruments. Unless you have a good deal of experience it is prudent to take and if necessary pay for a professional opinion. Cracked frames and soundboards or worn wrestplanks and loose tuning pins are common reasons for selling an old piano privately, and they are defects which take a great deal of time and money to correct even if you can find someone who will take the work on.

It is difficult to generalise further as to age and type. The oldest piano can be rebuilt, at great expense, to be a good instrument, but its sound may not be acceptable, and tastes in appearance vary widely. A piano from before about 1870, even if well restored, is unlikely to satisfy the seeker after a reasonably typical modern pianistic sound. Its frame will not stand modern tensions even if the piano is restrung and refelted throughout. From the early years of the twentieth century many fine pianos are now coming onto the market restored, and at least the structural material is likely to be of high quality if the make is well known. Modern felt and strings are likely to serve well even if they may be of less good quality than those originally fitted and beyond repair. A point to query is the size of the tuning pin head. It should fit a modern tuning lever. Pins which do not are inconvenient and in any case may well be loose. As to date, you may have to take the dealer's word with a dash of experience. If you can find the model number in the *Pierce Piano Atlas* (6th ed., 1965, available in the United Kingdom through musical supply houses), so much the better. As has been noted, one should have special reasons for buying an overdamped or straight strung upright, or any piano which does not have a full iron frame. As a general rule and bearing possible resale in mind, it is not advisable to buy a piano with a compass of less than seven octaves, though of course you might do so if fully aware of its limitations.

With regard to condition, note particularly any irregularity in touch and damping and insist that they be corrected. If they cannot be corrected, avoid the instrument. Raise the top of an upright and make sure that the hammer shanks are all lying even and flat on the hammer rail; if they are not, the action can probably be regulated to correct the fault—but should you buy from such a vendor (assuming that it is not a private purchase)? Similarly, with upright or grand, test that the dampers rise in a fairly straight line when the sustaining pedal is depressed, and that their rise is as much as the rise of one damper when a key is depressed. Insist that any squeaks and creaks in the pedal-work be seen to. Observe the tone of notes whose strings are either side of a bar in the frame; it may be too different from the general scale of tone in the instrument to be acceptable. Never buy a piano with a cracked frame or a cracked soundboard. These are radical defects, not always repairable, and they will not improve with age. Noticing a cracked frame (usually near the tuning pins) is a matter of close observation. Detecting a crack in the soundboard is made easier by shining a torch from behind (upright) or below (grand). The grand's soundboard is mostly visible from beneath. That of the upright is on older models usually covered by a sheet of cloth, and special care is then needed in the inspection. Be wary of buying a piano which is plainly or admittedly badly out of tune; you cannot quickly assess whether or not it can be made to hold its pitch in the future.

As it is up to the individual to complain if his piano is not properly maintained, or to do something constructive about it himself, so only he can select his instrument in the first place. We never have quite the money needed, and we are all out for a bargain, but with pianos it is best to buy as 'high' as you can (save possibly on the private market). The extra outlay is almost certain to be justified in quality, in durability or merely in terms of investment—the more expensive piano will still be worth more than its cheaper neighbour in years to come, for whatever reason. Musical taste is apt to develop in the owner, and playing a piano over whose choice you feel you made a mistake is a depressing experience.

PART TWO—CONSTRUCTION AND WORKING

3 Case and resonant parts

Case and structure

Basic structure of uprights and grands is similar in principle but the grand's case may be more involved in the quality of sound produced. (The upright case tends to shut in the sound if the lid is closed, of course.) Both pianos start from a framework of stout beams, the bottom or back of the instrument—the same frame which in earlier days carried the string tension. In the upright, this structure is four-sided with vertical and/or diagonal cross-beams. The external case members are attached to this self-contained carcass, which in modern pianos tends to be lighter than hitherto and without cross-beams as a fuller frame is used for support. In the grand, the ends of the beams, when suitably placed, are actually dovetailed into the sides of the case, and in particular into the long curved rim, which is usually made of ten or more compressed laminations continuing round to the back end of the straight side.

This wooden frame supports the iron frame, strings, keybed and action. In the grand, action and keyframe (on which the keys are balanced) are mounted together and merely rest on the (covered) beam structure extended beyond the rim into the straight sides at the front. The heavy iron frame rests, with the soundboard beneath it, on ledges round the rim and side or preferably on shelves formed by decreasing the wood's thickness from half way up. Thus on a grand the laminated rim is much thicker seen from below than it is seen from above. The wrest-

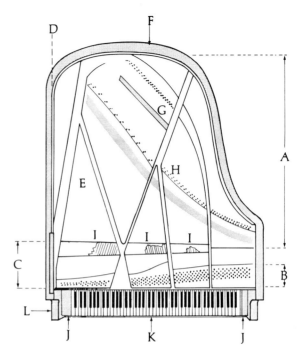

Fig. 16 Outline structure of grand piano

A Indicates area covered by soundboard
B Indicates area covered by wrestplank, below frame
C Indicates area occupied by the action
D End of laminated rim round curved side and end
E Bars of frame (shown by heavy line)
F Frame screwed over soundboard into thicker lower part of rim
G Bass overstrung bridge and hitchpins
H Long bridge and hitchpins
I Dampers at front edge of soundboard, just in front of which the hammers rise
J Keyblocks
K Keyslip
L Cheek

plank and frame are supported at the sides in front, but are somewhat weak, and should receive additional propping below when, for instance, tuning pins are driven in. The iron frame is screwed through into the beams, the screws being arranged to clear the soundboard which stands in the way (Figs. 16–17). In the upright, the whole frame is screwed into the beams and is of course uninterrupted by hammers. The wrestplank is also stuck to the top beam but the keybed, on which the keyframe and, behind it, the lower feet of the action rest, has to be at right-angles. It is therefore fitted with side-pieces known as cheeks. These are screwed into the case sides and, in older models, into columns rising from the short projecting beams ('toe-blocks') at each corner of the case, to which castors are fitted (Fig. 18). The legs of grands are detachable and are screwed or clamped in various ways to the rim, side and beams. The upright's action is usually fitted at the top to bolts passing through the iron frame and into the beams, but the various alternative methods of mounting will be plain from observation. Sometimes central metal support straps of metal are also used.

In both upright and grand the soundboard is between the frame and the beams, into which its projecting ribs are dovetailed behind or below. In the upright it continues unbroken up to the wrest-plank, though considerable corners may be cut off to prevent any tendency of a large board to vibrate in separate parts (Fig. 18). In the grand it rests between the frame and the rim and side ledges, so being closely tied into the case. It covers the whole rear part of the piano (whose shape of course already represents a cut-off corner) but has to stop short towards the front where the hammers rise (Figs. 16–17). The sides and the bars of the frame continue past this gap to the wrestplank, which may be covered

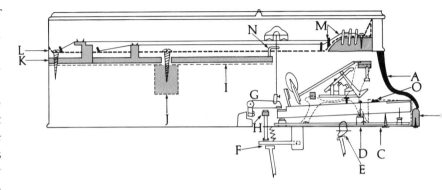

Fig. 17 Section through grand piano
A Fall
B Keyslip
C Keyblock (within broken line)
D Centre (balance) rail of keyframe
E Soft pedal mechanism acting on keyframe
F Sustaining pedal mechanism
G Damper lever
H Damper rail
I Broken line indicates thicker rim to support frame and soundboard
J One of the bottom beams, with screw from frame through soundboard
K Soundboard and bridges (shaded)
L Frame (heavy broken line)
M Wrestplank (shaded), agraffes and frame
N Damper rod guide with bushings
O Strip to prevent keys from rising

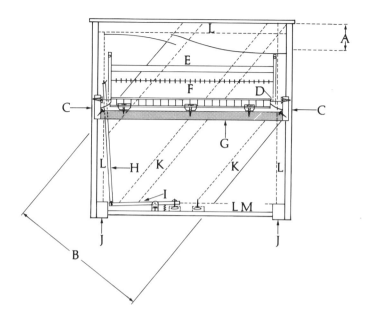

Fig. 18 Outline structure of older upright piano

A Indicates approximate area of wrestplank (beneath frame)
B Indicates approximate area of soundboard
C Cheeks
D Keyblock
E Hammer rail
F Location of the checks
G Keybed, to which is screwed keyframe
H Soft pedal rod
I Soft pedal lever (sustaining pedal work not shown)
J Toeblocks
K Back beams, use of which depends on fullness and strength of iron frame
L Basic structural back beams
M Toerail (at front), if present

by the pierced casting or left open but supported by the top of the frame. Like cracks in a soundboard, any deterioration of the join between soundboard and case or beams should be viewed with the greatest suspicion. It can be remedied, but not easily, and it may indicate deformity in the soundboard.

Access within

Access inside an upright is by removing the front panels. The top front panel usually has short dowels locating in holes in the fall bar, and catches mounted on top of the case sides, these being visible when the top lid is opened. Thus the panel is removed by unfastening the catches and lifting upwards and forwards. The action can then easily be unscrewed, but care should be taken first to separate it from the pedal rods to the left (and, occasionally, to the right). The lower panel is similarly dowelled into the toe-rail (through which the pedals emerge) and is held by various forms of spring latch at the top so that it stays in place below the keybed. Removal forwards exposes the pedal trapwork, hitch-pins and lower parts of the bridges.

Access into a grand is less convenient. As a rule the fall (i.e. the keyboard lid) must first be removed. It is usually fitted merely with pins locating in metal pivot blocks in the cheeks, so that it can be lifted out upwards once the precise direction of movement is found. This will reveal the keys, and the action deep inside. To go further involves taking off the keyslip, which is generally fitted with locating dowels in the front edge of the case and held down at each end by overlapping parts of the keyblocks at each side of the keyboard. Alternatively, it may be screwed in from below. Most often, the blocks are fitted by large screws or bolts from beneath the piano, but sometimes they are screwed in from the sides (as is general in uprights) below the level of the keys (some of which must therefore be removed) or from above by screws covered by felt or rubber buttons which can be pressed out. In grands there is invariably a slip of felted wood holding the keys in case they should jump up their pins on the return of the hammers. This slip has to be removed before extreme keys can be taken out with a view to moving side-screwed keyblocks. In due course, when the keyslip and blocks are out, keyboard and action slide forwards—they are heavy, so proceed warily, ensuring that no hammers are up at the time. The damper mechanism and connection with the pedals will be visible once the action is removed.

Resonant parts

The case and other elements of course vibrate in varying degree, but the principal resonant parts other than the strings themselves are the soundboard and bridges. The latter transmit vibrations of strings to the soundboard, which vibrates a large mass of air and so amplifies the sound of the strings.

We have already referred to the partial vibrations of strings, and from this fact that vibrations extend far beyond a string's fundamental pitch follows the necessity for extreme speed in transmission of vibrations over the whole soundboard. This has determined that soundboards are almost universally made of wood, usually spruce, fir or pine, though other materials have been tried. The average thickness is about 7mm but opinion differs as to whether boards should be of constant thickness or have a taper, The large area is composed of several planks glued together and with their grain running parallel to the bridges, in practice some 50° to the vertical or central line of the instrument. In modern pianos the strength of glues permits the boards to be glued edge-to-

edge. Soundboards are domed upwards (by degrees of heat shrinkage and by fixing them to pre-shaped ribs) towards the strings and then glued all round to the rim, edge and beams. The doming amounts to about 5mm in an average upright. The ribs serve the purpose of support, but are also essential to transmission of vibration across the grain of the soundboard. They are tapered towards the ends and these are lodged in beams or rim.

A sunken soundboard requires factory attention and reconditioning it may not be economic. Repairing a soundboard which is cracked or whose joints have sprung is sometimes possible but always chancy. If inspection reveals flaws and chinks it is prudent not to buy the piano, for the likelihood is that its tone will always be thin and repair will be costly. At the worst, one can fill cracks with hard-setting animal glue and fillets of veneer and this will produce some improvement. Some hairline cracks are fairly harmless, however—it is best to take advice if you own a piano with old fine cracks.

The strings, according to the 'bearing' imposed by pressure bar or agraffes at the wrestplank end, and to the height of the hitchpin frame at the other end, press down onto the bridges and are kept in close contact by bridge pins (Fig. 1). These are placed to divert the strings in alternate directions from a straight path and are angled at some 70° to prevent rattle and jumping. They must be entirely firm in the bridges and are driven into the hard beech or maple bridge-top for about two-thirds of their length. The edges of bridges are carefully cut at angles to ensure a precise start to the speaking lengths of the strings.

Bridge construction varies according to the design of the frame. In grands the 'long bridge' (whose underside is of course curved to match the belly of the domed soundboard) is nearly uninterrupted, since bracing bars pass above most of it, and it may indeed be continuous with only slight cut-outs for the bars. In uprights the bars must be closer to the soundboard (because of the action's position) and the bridge is often broken completely at these points. Then a block is screwed and glued to the end of each section behind the soundboard to counteract the gap, though frequently there is still a perceptible difference of tone around the frame bars. There is always a separate, higher, bridge for the overstrung strings and this is usually suspended, that is, has an overhang (Fig. 17), so that a longer speaking length can be given to these strings even though the bridge cannot be placed too near to the edge of the soundboard. Bridges are ideally fixed to soundboards by glue and dowels only, but screws also are often used, with wooden washers behind to spread the strain over the thin wood. The pressure of the strings and height of the bridges are important to tone, and a sunken soundboard is a common cause of thin tone in elderly instruments.

No repair in this area is easy and all are fraught with the danger of spoiling the sound. There are a few smaller jobs which the owner may be able to carry out, however. The filling of cracks in the soundboard has already been mentioned. Loose ribs or edges to the soundboard can be reglued under pressure (though it is unwise to try to remove the soundboard itself). Loose bridges can be tightened by their screws (or temporary screws may be put in for the purpose) and glued. Unless a new cap can be obtained for a bridge, repinning it is a radical step (see Chapter 6, 'Notes rattle, whistle or ring') but may be inevitable if the pins have broken up the whole surface. It is worth trying to tap odd pins in further (after loosening the strings) before resorting to a more thorough job. The varnish given to soundboards and the sides (never the tops) of bridges is protective and does not affect the sound, but obviously renewal, for instance with clear polyurethane lacquer, is desirable and not difficult if you are doing some renovation of an old piano. Repairs and adjustments to stringing are considered in Chapter 6 below.

The cautionary note should perhaps be added that repairs to the resonant side of a piano usually involve removing the strings. This is not in itself difficult but should be done by a system which will not result in a sudden release of tension in part of the frame. Any order for making release gradual will do; what is not desirable is to take off each string from top to bottom or from bottom to top. Further, removal of the strings may well reveal, if it does not cause, more extensive flaws than were known to exist. For example, old strings may break or tuning pins be found to be loose. Ways of dealing with such situations are mentioned in Chapter 6, but it is as well to be prepared for them before undertaking the job. Attempting a repair in this area is, inevitably, more far-reaching than is, for example, trying to correct faulty action of one note. You will not know the outcome until you have restrung and reassembled the instrument, and then you will have to be prepared for some time to elapse before it will hold the pitch to which it is retuned.

8 **Upright piano backs** Modern braceless back on small piano

9 **Upright piano backs** Modern braced back

10 **Upright piano backs** Braced back of an old straight strung piano

4 Action, keyboard and pedals

The action

Most piano actions differ little so far as the layman is concerned, and to help in understanding them composite, non-specific, examples of types for uprights and grands will be used. If the principles of these are clear, departures and differences, particularly in older actions, can be understood from observation. It is not always easy to imagine, from a drawing of the static action at rest, how the positions of the various parts will change when the action is in use and a narrative can be long and complicated. Therefore in the following pages the positions of actions at important stages in key-depression are illustrated and a brief commentary is given. Accepted names of parts are set out in the first diagram of each series and broad guides as to regulation are given at the end of each section.

A general word should be said here on regulation. To regulate an action is to bring all its parts into adjustment to achieve the desired objectives with the greatest mechanical efficiency. It is primarily a case of relating the behaviour of keys, hammers and dampers on the lines of accepted standards, which may be slightly modified to personal taste, particularly where touch is concerned. The touch is, of course, normally heavier towards the bass, but the change should be entirely gradual. The well-regulated action gives maximum impulse to the hammers yet does not permit them to bounce or block on the strings, together with consistently timed, but not obtrusive, action of the dampers. An action where hammer felts are worn and trenched, or where the hammer shanks are deeply embedded in the hammer rail felt, needs the hammers brought closer to the strings. Regulation is again needed if the felts are renewed. A generally worn action will allow escapement to occur early, so that power is wasted. Poor damper regulation produces lingering sounds, strings clogged by dampers, and uneven touch. Slack jack regulation produces sloppy, clicking keys even if the key bushings are in good order. Worn or misplaced checks lead to poor repetition, as does maladjustment of the springs in a grand repetition action. Regulation (which is ideally a systematic procedure carried throughout but may also be limited to obviously offending notes) affects the whole performance of the instrument, both in touch and in sound.

The measurements given in the notes on regulating are guides. They are generally applicable, especially for more modern instruments, but with a worn piano compromises have to be made, either in them or in how far general performance is to be lowered to the best that can be done with the worst (normally the middle) notes. Whatever standards are found best by experiment, they must then be followed consistently throughout or the instrument will be no pleasure to play. Further notes on some of the details of regulating will be found in Chapter 6.

The upright action

Fig. i At rest

Note that the weight of the hammer rests on the hammer rail, not on the jack and so not on the key. The tip of the jack is a thin card's distance from the acting surface of the butt. The bridle tape is straight or almost straight, but not tightly stretched.

A Hammer head
B Hammer shank
C Hammer rail, divided or otherwise arranged so that it can be swung forward by action of the soft pedal
D Hammer butt, with padded leather acting surface and felt pad beneath the resting jack
E Back stop
F Hammer check
G Bridle tape
H Bridle wire
I Wippen, with felt or foot to engage key capstan
J Jack, pivoted on wippen and sprung beneath foot
K Regulating button, screwed into a regulating rail (not shown) attached to the frame, and engaging with jack foot
L Alternative forms of jack stop (not always present); a jack slap rail or an extension to the back stop
M Damper slap rail (not always present) which bears one form of hammer spring acting on the butt
N Alternative form of hammer spring, anchored to butt and catching in silk loop fastened to hammer flange
O Damper spoon
P Damper lever and felted tail to engage spoon
Q Sustaining rod engaging with damper tail

R Damper spring
S Damper head, clamped to damper wire and fastened through felt to damper
T Damper

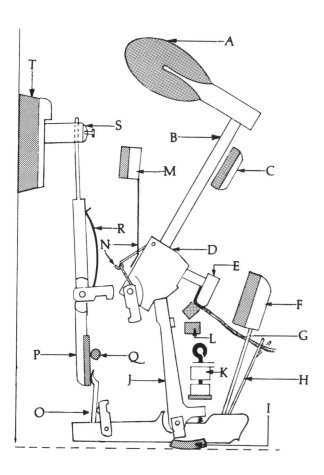

The action at rest

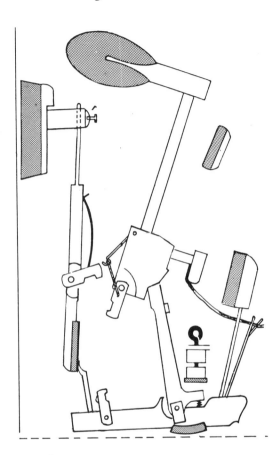

Fig. ii Damper rises

The key is depressed about 3mm and the hammer is about half-way to the string when the spoon engages the damper tail and forces the damper off the string against its spring. The jack is driving the hammer butt and its foot is approaching the regulating button. The tape is slack.

Damper rises

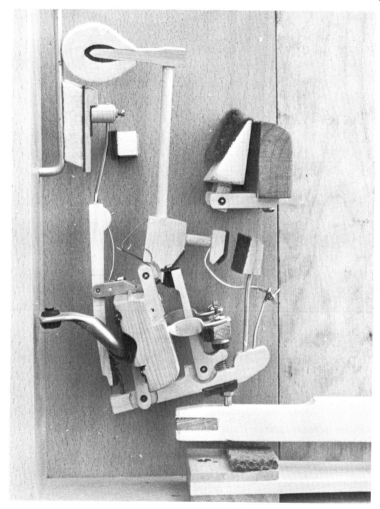

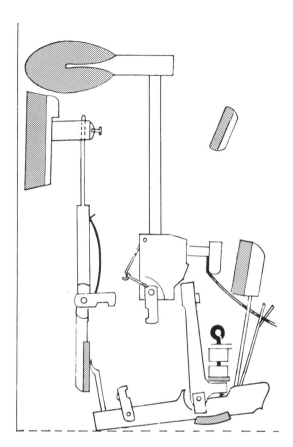

Fig. iii Escapement

Regulating button and jack foot have engaged, forcing jack tip away from
hammer butt. The hammer is some 2mm from the string and is moving by
impetus, being detached from the jack. The tape is slack as the hammer
approaches and strikes the key, but will tighten when the wippen falls,
on key release, and hammer follows. The key will depress some 1mm
further.

Escapement

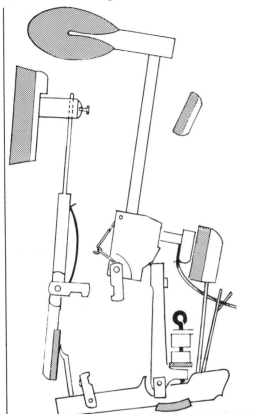

Fig. iv Return and check

The hammer stop is arrested by the check whilst the damper is raised and the jack disengaged, if the key is held down. The tape remains slack. When the key is released, the wippen falls, the tape comes taut and jerks the hammer to the hammer rail, and the jack falls into place beneath the hammer butt. (If the key is struck and released quickly, these two phases of return are not distinct.)

The check position

Lost motion at jack when soft pedal depressed

Regulation of upright action

1 Check that hammer heads are 50mm from the strings when at rest. Increase rail felt or bring action forward if necessary.
2 Adjust key capstan screws so that the jack tips are a thin card's thickness away from the hammer butts, all the hammers being squarely back against the hammer rail and the key fronts being up.
3 Ensure that the tapes are straight but not taut when the action is at rest. Adjust by bending the bridle wires. Try to arrange that the tapes do not quite move the wippens when the soft pedal is depressed.
4 Remove the action and check that no damper is held back by its tail's resting on the damper spoon. Bend spoons to release where needed. Replace the action and ensure that the strings are fully damped when the action is at rest, bending the damper wires when necessary. Depress the sustaining pedal and bend damper wires until all the dampers rise to clear the strings in a straight line. For each key, check that the damper moves when the key is depressed 2–3mm and the hammer is half-way to the string. Identify and bend in towards the action frame any damper spoons where dampers move early. Do the reverse with dampers which move late. Repeat as necessary.
5 Arrange for escapement to occur with the hammer heads as close to the strings as possible (normally about 2mm), so long as it does occur reliably. Adjust by screwing the regulating button up or down with a slotted screwdriver or similar tool.
6 Bend the checks so that the hammers are caught some 20mm from the strings after escapement, when keys are held down after striking.
7 Adjust pedal lever screws so that the pedals have about 8mm free movement.
8 Set the movable hammer rail (by screws if adjustable, or by felt washers on the rod and by the lever screw if not) to give acceptable soft pedal action with minimal movement of resting keys when the pedal is depressed.

The grand action

Fig. v At rest

The hammer is held clear of the hammer rail, its weight resting on the repetition lever and so on the key. The repetition lever is sprung up against its stop. The jack is aligned with the wood fillet in the centre of the hammer roller, but the repetition lever holds the roller slightly higher than the tip of the jack.

A Damper

B Damper wire passing through felted bush guide

C Damper lever (weighted)

D Key with felted tip to engage with damper lever

E Capstan screw

F Check and wire fixed to key

G Wippen

H Jack, pivoted at end of wippen and with tip passing through slot in end of repetition lever

I Regulating button

J Jack stop button, adjustable to set jack's depth of engagement with hammer roller

K Repetition lever, pivoted and sprung to wippen

L Repetition lever stop button, adjusting height of lever to the jack tip when at rest

M Repetition lever spring (design varies), adjustable with a set-screw and here engaging with a silk loop passing through the lever and attached to the wippen

N Jack spring (design varies), passing through slots to engage with silk loop on the jack.

O Hammer

P Hammer rail or rest, fitted to frame and with adjustable height

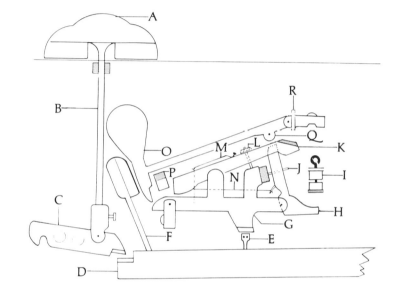

Q Hammer roller (or knuckle) of felt and leather with wooden core, against which the jack acts to drive the hammer

R Drop screw or hammer shank flange regulating screw, setting the height to which the repetition lever will rise when the key is depressed

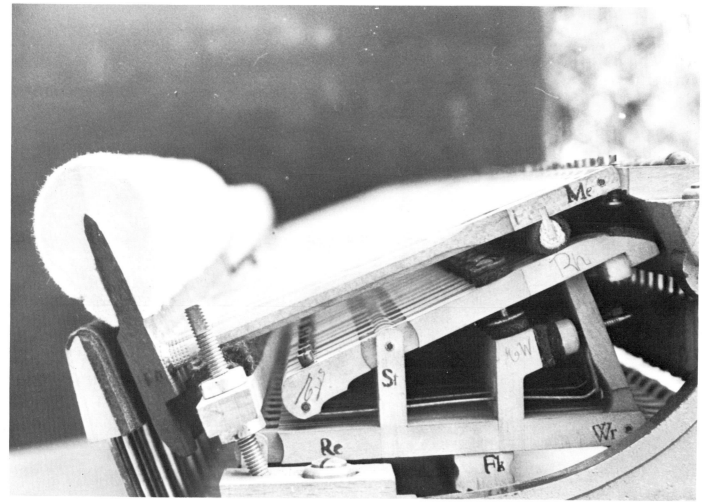

The action at rest

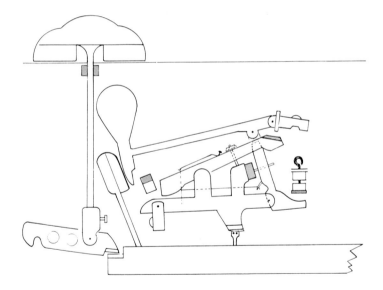

Damper rises

Fig. vi Damper rises
The key is depressed about 3mm and the hammer is half-way to the string, when the tip of the key engages with the damper lever and starts to raise the damper. The hammer is driven, on the roller, by the jack, through the slot in the repetition lever.

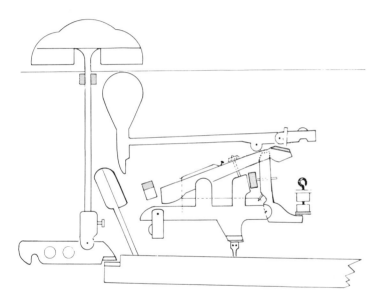

Fig. vii Escapement
The heel of the jack has met the regulating button and the tip of the jack has been forced away from the hammer roller. The repetition lever is stopped by the drop screw and the hammer roller drops back onto the lever, whose spring then cushions its return.

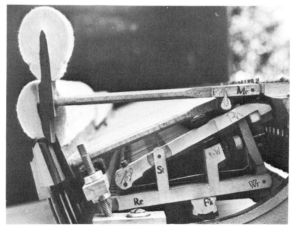

(i) Escapement
(ii) 'Drop' position (if key depressed lightly and held down)

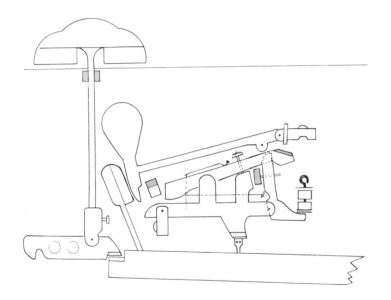

Fig. viii Return (a)

The falling hammer depresses the repetition lever against its spring and
falls until the back of the head is caught by the check, so long as the key is
held down. The jack remains disengaged from the hammer roller.

Check

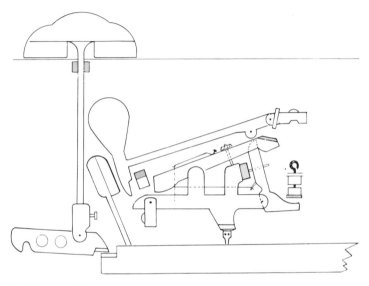

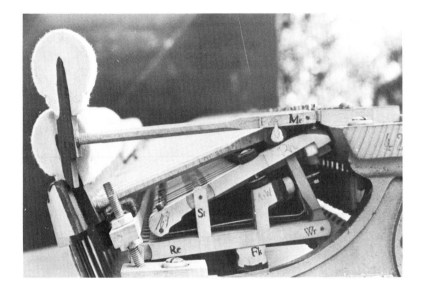

Fig. ix Return (b)

At the slightest release of the key, the spring of the repetition lever raises the hammer, which is released by the check as the key front rises. The jack is then relocated beneath the hammer roller even if the key is not fully released.

If the key is immediately released after striking, the hammer brushes over the check and bottoms on the hammer rail, from which the lever restores it to the normal slightly raised rest position as the key comes level, and the jack is similarly relocated.

Raising hammer by repetition lever on part release of key

Regulation of grand action

1 Adjust key capstans until hammer heads are 50mm from the strings, and set hammer rail to be 3mm below the hammer shanks when this strike distance has been obtained.

2 By means of jack stops and springs, set the tips of the jacks just in front of the wooden fillets in the hammer rollers—slight depression of the repetition levers will be needed to make this adjustment, and the wippens must be held meanwhile.

By means of stop pads, regulate the repetition levers so that they hold the hammer rollers out of touch, by a thin card's thickness, of the jack tips. Check that the hammer heads are still 50mm from the strings and readjust as necessary.

3 By pressing down onto the strings, make sure that the dampers are resting fully on them when the action is at rest. Have the dampers rise in a straight line when the sustaining pedal is depressed, allowing 2mm between the lever raising rail and the damper levers. Adjust with damper wire grub-screws or, for the pedal, with felt or paper washers on the raising rail. Arrange, by thinning or thickening the felt on the key tips, or by adjusting the lever grubscrews, for the dampers to rise when the keys are depressed 2–3mm or the hammers are half-way up.

4 Let escapement occur with the hammer heads as close to the strings as possible (normally 2mm) so long as it does occur reliably. Adjust by screwing the regulating button up or down.

5 Depressing the keys gently and holding them down, adjust the drop of the hammers onto the repetition levers to 2mm, by turning the drop screw.

6 Depress the keys harder (but not enough to send the hammers far above horizontal, or they may be damaged) and hold them down. Bend the checks until they catch the hammers at 20mm from the strings but do not touch the hammers as they move up to strike.

7 Half-release the hammers after they have been checked, and regulate the rising of the hammers by adjustment of the repetition lever springs, so that there is positive but not bouncing rise. Ensure that the jacks relocate, and very slightly let off the repetition lever stop pads of any which do not.

8 Adjust the key-retaining strip to allow about 2mm upward movement of the key fronts from rest position.

9 Adjust the pedal connecting rods to give about 8mm of free movement.

10 Set the stops in the treble key block and key-frame to ensure correct alignment of hammers and strings when the soft pedal is fully depressed.

The keyboard

Keys are laid on a frame comprising three rails, one or more central members, and endpieces (Fig. 19). The middle rail, known as the 'balance rail', serves as a fulcrum and is screwed with pins on which the keys centre. The back rail is covered with baize felt. The front rail has an oval pin for each key and, round the pins, baize and paper washers, the baize being a cushioning stop for the key and the paper washers, which are also used on the balance pins, being for adjustment of key height and touch depth ('key dip'). The oval pins are for limiting sideways movements of the key front; on a new piano these pins are virtually in line with the keys but, as the bushings wear, the pins can be turned to take up the slack. Where nowadays there are sometimes plastic (rather than felt) bushings in the keys, round rather than oval pins may be used in the front rail on the assumption that these bushings will not wear or compress.

Keys are merely dropped into place on the pins, although grand keyboards have a slip screwed some 2mm over the keys to prevent them from excessive jumping on the return of the hammers. The full dip of the keys is set at 10mm, and the washers must be adjusted so that this dip is available when the keys are as level as possible when at rest. If, for example, additional papers are put on the central balance pin to raise up too low a key, paper will also be needed on the oval pin at the front, or the raising of the key would result in an increase beyond standard key dip. Relaying a keyboard level, and with correct dip and sideways freedom, is not difficult (though time-consuming) even with improvised washers of punched felt and paper.

The assembled keyframe is screwed into the keybed of an upright, and removal of some keys will be necessary to reveal the

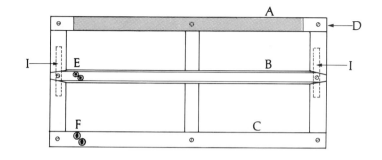

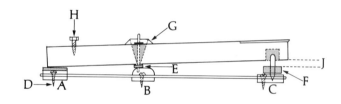

Fig. 19 Keyframe and (upright) key in section
A Back rail, felted
B Centre or balance rail
C Front rail
D Screws fixing keyframe to keybed
E Centre rail balance pins with felt washers
F Oval front rail pins with washers
G Chase fits over cut-out in key and retains cloth bushing
H Capstan screw
I Shows where action frame is screwed in a grand
J Key dip (actually measured between adjacent keys)

63

securing screws. In a grand with normal 'shift' soft-pedal system, the key-frame, together with the action, is not secured but merely limited in movement. At the bass side it is limited by a block fixed to the case and, at the treble side, by the pedal spring and an adjustable stop-screw in the righthand keyblock. At the back it rests against set blocks or adjustable screws, and in front it may touch the keyslip.

Keys are nowadays of standard size. Their proportions are closely related to the action so that there is correct leverage, represented by the small key-dip and comparatively large swing of the hammer. This leverage is largely attributable to the hammer, for the tail of the key in fact moves less than the front (Fig. 5). In uprights, there are three parts in front of the balance pin and two parts behind. In grands the active part of the key is proportioned with two parts in front of the balance pin and one part between balance pin and capstan. The same proportions and leverage apply to the black keys, known as 'sharps', of which the leverage is somewhat less. The sharps are usually laid to be about 12mm higher (at the front) than the naturals. The proportions of keys are such, and the bushings are so contrived, that any key is horizontal when half-depressed. According to how far the key extends behind the capstan, it tends to tip back when at rest without the action, but this varies considerably. The poise is set for a particular action and it is a mistake to try to alter it although occasional weighting or lightening of a key may be justified where the key is irregular for no apparent reason. Weights are often sunk into the tails of keys to encourage more strong backward balance if this is required. The keys of grands, however, tend to be weighted at the front to compensate for the weight of the hammers which they carry when at rest.

The poise of keys is of course an important element in a piano's touch. In standard terms acceptable touch exists when the key (with action) can be fully depressed by a weight of 55–85gm, usually nearer 85gm in the bass. As has been noted already, instruments meeting this standard may nonetheless give very different sensations of touch according as to where the resistance is principally located (in the action, or in the inertia of the keys, in damper springs or in hammer weights and springs) and at what stages in the keys' descent these resistances are encountered.

Modern white keys are covered in ivorine, or various white gloss plastics. These coverings are in one piece on top and, often, also at the front. Older ivory keys are invariably in three pieces, one from the back to the front of the sharps, one from the sharps to the edge, and the third for the front. It is extremely difficult to match old key covers and, short of recovering the whole keyboard, which may be a pity as well as a big undertaking, one can only compromise by roughening and then tinting a suitable white plastic. Modern whites are thicker than old coverings and to fit them usually involves reducing the wood of the keys concerned. For both ivory and substitutes the proverbial milk and water are good cleaners, while metal polish will do a more drastic job. On ivory a toothpowder mixed with glycerine to a stiff paste may be tried. Methylated spirits is also an effective cleaner and tripoli mixed with oil will smooth a rough surface but leave it matt.

The keys all end in a 'capstan' (other names are also used) which forms an adjustable connection with the action. In a modern piano where space is limited the capstan is generally some form of brass screw adjustable either with a spanner or having holes to receive a prong for turning it. Older capstans are higher, being dowels (with similar holes for turning) mounted on fixed screws.

These are capped with felt, whilst for metal capstans the low foot of the wippen is felted instead. In older pianos, again, connection might be with a pivoted arm attached to the action frame and wippen and known as the 'abstract', rather than with the wippen directly. Abstracts are also used in mini-pianos where much of the action is below the level of the keyboard. For regulation of the connection between key and action see 'Touch' in Chapter 6.

The pedals

The various pedal systems have already been outlined (Chapter 1), but something must be said of their construction and working.

Pedals of uprights are pivoted either below or above the bottom boards of the case and project through holes in the toe-rail. The springing is in the bottom of the case and, broadly, there are two systems. In one, the pedals are attached by adjustable screws to levers going (usually) to the left, and which are fixed to leaf-springs whose other ends are fitted to the bottom boards. In this arrangement, the spring also acts as the pivot of the lever. In the other arrangement, levers and attachment to the pedals are similar, but the end of the lever nearest to the pedal rests on a coiled spring, and the lever is pivoted on a steel pin passing through it and into a block screwed to the bottom board (Plate 11). In either case (and whether for soft or sustaining pedal) we have the outside end of a lever raised by the depression of the pedal. This rising end locates with a rod going up the side of the piano and operating the sustaining rod or the hammer rail in the action. Adjustment of the point at which the pedal has effect is principally by tightening or slackening the screw which connects pedal and lever. It is usual to allow slightly less than a centimetre's lost motion before any effect

is produced by depressing either pedal. There are many variations of detail, but these are the basic systems.

The grand's pedals are of course in a lyre or plainer type of trapwork suspension beneath the piano and are connected by metal rods going upwards to the action and damper levers. A cardinal difference from the upright is that the grand has no intermediate lever. Consequently, its pedals are pivoted so that the backs swing up when the fronts are depressed (whereas the pedals of the upright are pivoted at the end, not midway). The grand's soft pedal rod contacts some form of hinged arm in the keybed, the other end of which locates with a central bar of the keyframe and shifts keys and action to the right when the pedal is depressed (Fig. 10a). The only spring is the powerful leafspring pressing against the keyframe and screwed into the righthand cheek of the case. The spring of the sustaining pedal is a downward bearing coil spring acting on a tongue or flap which is pushed by the connecting rod. This tongue, which will be found under the piano behind where the rods enter, is joined to a short dowel which goes up inside the piano to raise the damper rail, a strip of wood passing immediately below the damper levers and raising them simultaneously when lifted (Fig. 9). The grand's pedals should be set to have similar lost motion to those of the upright. They are adjusted usually by nuts which have the effect of shortening or lengthening the rods at the top. Alternatively, washers can be added at various points of contact and wear on the leather pads at the back ends of the pedals can be made good. In principle, this lost motion is a matter of safety; there must be no chance of the dampers being held off the strings when the pedals are not in use. In practice, of course, it is a matter of convention and pianos incorrectly adjusted here seem to react very strangely to footwork.

11 **Arrangements for upright piano pedals** (above) Arrangement with
leaf spring (here soft pedal lever and rod go to right)
Arrangements for upright piano pedals (below) Arrangement with
lever pivot blocks and coil springs

PART THREE—MAINTENANCE

5 Tuning and toning

Tuning requirement

Retailers and tuners differ in the frequency of tuning which they recommend for domestic pianos. This is inevitable, since several factors—use, the stability and past history of the instrument, the heating and environment, the particularity of the owner—vary widely. There cannot really be a general rule. What the owner should bear in mind is that the less often a piano is tuned the more work is likely to be needed when the time comes. This work cannot reasonably be done at the same cost or in the same time as a more routine tuning session. The tuner may not know the condition of the instrument at all when he makes an appointment, and he cannot necessarily fit in extra time even if the owner is prepared to pay. The result of too infrequent tuning is likely to be dissatisfaction on both sides.

To try to cut tuning costs is false economy on the owner's part. Of course there is no point in paying far above the going rate for an ordinary job, but the tuner who has to drum up business by charging an exceptionally low price must be some-what suspect. Again, in an annual visit what should be done may not be done. In general, a modern piano in conditions which do not vary much ought to be tuned at least twice, and preferably three times, a year. A sensitive owner would benefit from three or four tunings of his piano—he will find that an apparent gradual deterioration of tone is in fact a loss of edge in the tuning. In addition, pianos need tuning after they have been moved. A new piano should be tuned on arrival and a month or two afterwards. A restrung piano, if it is holding its pitch reasonably well after initial tunings, will probably need tuning some three times in its first six to nine months and by then should have settled. For an established piano, there is a certain sense in seasonal tunings, but it has to be remembered that the profession tends to be under heavy pressure of work before the start of school terms.

What is involved in tuning? There is the setting of a starting point in relation to an agreed pitch—it may be concert pitch (in which the A over Middle C has a frequency of 440 cycles a second) or lower, depending on the age of the piano and whether it is to be used for accompanying other instruments tuned to that pitch, or voices used to it. Increasing the overall pitch of a piano by only a semitone greatly raises internal stress, so bringing up pitch has to be done gradually over several sessions, and a tuner has to judge whether an instrument made before the adoption of this standard pitch (and consequently for one of the earlier and mainly lower pitch standards) will tolerate raising. Secondly, every interval on the piano must be accurately related to that starting-point, that is the piano must be in tune as well as up to pitch. There are, of course, mathematically correct intervals, but they do not neces-sarily sound correct on individual instruments, because of varying harmonic quality, and it is the tuner's art to tune a particular instrument with regard to its merits and limitations as well as to theoretical requirements.

Unless they suffer from or are blessed with an uncommonly accurate sense of pitch related to the scale gradations which we use, most owners are happy for a piano to be reasonably near to standard pitch. They are far more sensitive to incorrect octaves, other intervals, and 'unisons' (strings of a bichord or trichord)—it is here that a piano is first felt to be 'out of tune' or merely to 'sound funny'. Some tuners in a hurry thus spend little time on the pitch or the crucial intervals in the octave or so surrounding the starting note (on which the whole tuning is based) but agree the unisons in that middle octave and then tune the lower and higher octaves to match. This will certainly improve things as a quick touch-up, but at least once a year the piano must be properly tuned throughout with a new 'bearing' (this central core of notes) laid, or error will pile on error.

If a piano is allowed to become very badly out, not only will it take longer to tune, but it may not hold the tuning which it is given. The frame, soundboard and bridges set in a habitual disposition and the strings bend most readily where they have been bent before. In course of time, fatigue sets in at these points (and by the tuning pins and agraffes) and tuning the piano may well cause broken strings. If you buy or otherwise come by an old piano, you take a risk in buying it untuned. If it has been regularly tuned, so much the better, but at least if you buy it more or less in tune you know that it can be tuned and that it will hold its tuning for more than five minutes.

Tuners

The piano-owning public seem generally to know nothing about tuning and to regard the tuner as a necessary evil or one with sacred but inexplicable mysteries to hand. Tuners are chosen largely on recommendation and partly on price. Price is no guide and recommendation is often unreliable, being from an owner whose piano presents problems quite other than one's own and whose standards may not be very high. Nothing but wider knowledge and even practice of tuning can improve this situation. The tuner need not in fact be 'musical' (i.e. a latent performer) and may sound distinctly heavy-handed. He is in fact the better for being heavy in his tuning touch and he does not need to be a pianist in order to tune—though some competence might help to get over the very considerable difficulty of communication between owners and tuners who may seem unappreciative of pianistic complaints and shortcomings.

When he strikes a note, the tuner is not merely hearing how things sound but also performing a mechanical operation for which a delicate touch is unsuited. This is because the tension imported to the wrestpin must be evenly distributed throughout the string, despite the obstacles of agraffes and bridge pins, or the string will go flat before it has been played many times. There is a whole empirical science of 'setting' a tuning pin—moving it and evening up the tension in such a way that the string will stay at the desired new tension throughout. Again, if your tuner voices or otherwise adjusts the piano, his touch may seem inartistic, perhaps using the same finger on every note without variation of force. The tuner, however, is really concerned with consistent results from a consistent touch. Playing a varied romantic piece will not help him to decide what is irregular or obtrusive. Moreover, he must adjust to the player in general. He can hardly, and should not need to, adjust to idiosyncrasies of the individual's touch unless for a special reason asked to do so. If, of course, he can in the end play to you musically, even if only his set piece, your confidence will be increased; one does sometimes wish that tuners would show more affinity with the piano as an instrument for expression and enjoyment.

The basis of tuning

There are manuals on tuning and the reader who is interested may pursue the theory and practice there. For the present purpose the following is merely a description of the main processes which may whet the appetites of some readers and perhaps usefully inform others. At the very least, it can be helpful to know what your tuner is doing and why. Seemingly, the problem which confronts the tuner is how to construct between 71 and 87 intervals (according to the piano's compass) from one note provided by a tuning fork or other source. It is solved basically by the phenomena of harmonics and the presence or absence of 'beats'.

To the practised ear the second harmonic of a string is very audible an octave higher than its fundamental frequency. (To the unpractised ear it may be brought out by playing a note of a tuned piano, holding it down, and silently depressing the key an octave higher, when the harmonic of the first note will in fact cause the strings an octave higher to sound in sympathy. This is most easily tried in the tenor range of the piano.) The interval of a fifth (the third harmonic, an octave and a fifth above the fundamental) is also perceptible. These two intervals of an octave and a fifth are 'perfect'—their upper frequencies are integral multiples of the fundamental frequency, and the higher two strings are a half and a third of the length of the first string (provided that they are of the same qualities and tension).

Now the requirement of the accepted keyboard is to divide each octave into twelve exactly equal parts. Unhappily, the twelve harmonics (or notes derived therefrom) do not provide such equal divisions when translated back into the octave range of the first frequency and do not even add up to a perfect octave. All except the fifth are considerably out, and even the perfect fifth has to be flattened (when ascending the scale) to correspond to an equal division. Thus the 'pure' harmonic intervals have to be 'tempered' so that all semitone intervals are the same, save that the octave itself is retained pure and untempered in the tuned piano. Imperfect and tempered intervals are felt as a number of beats (effectively ebbs and flows of sound) to each interval in the time of a second, and a tuner is trained to sense the beats in musical intervals as the sound dies away, beats which become slower as you approach a perfect interval and faster as you move away from it. Thus the tuner comes correctly to flatten the upper notes of fifths and to make the upper notes of sixths sharp (and so on), so that all semitone intervals are, subject to small deviations which may be required for each piano, equal, and a piece can be played in any key with recognisably correct intervals.

There are several ways of 'laying the bearing'—establishing a basis of at least an octave's range in the middle of the piano (where beats are most easily heard). They involve going round in a cycle of restricted intervals (most often fifths and fourths, sometimes also thirds) until, taking an octave up or down where necessary to contain the exercise, the note an octave above or below the first note is reached. If this does not sound as a true and beatless octave, some of the temperament is wrong and steps have to be retraced. Once the bearing is laid, the tuner works up and down, primarily but not entirely in perfect octaves, to tune the rest of the piano. In some ways it is best to do the bass first so that any increased tension here may exert its 'see-saw' influence on the treble before the higher more sensitive strings are tuned, otherwise the precise tuning of the treble can be upset by subsequent tuning of the bass, but practice varies in this respect. One string at a time must be tuned and therefore rubber or felt mutes are used to silence other strings of bichords and trichords. Some prefer to tune most of the piano using a single continuous strip of felt placed between strings so that the whole instrument is tuned on single strings and then the others, the unisons, are attended to afterwards. This has the advantage of eliminating sympathetic vibrations from strings which are not struck, and of laying the tension evenly over the whole range before increasing it by adding other strings.

Your own tuning?

The piano owner can only by long practice tune his piano by ear, and in the course of the practice he may well make his instrument unplayable and incur the disfavour of the professional tuner. Improvements can, however, be made where the piano is not badly out and unattended, and experience can, more slowly, be gained in this way. In particular, unisons and octaves can be corrected by testing strings at intervals of an octave to determine which are correct and then tuning the others to match. You will have to employ a mute, because you must tune single strings (not notes) to each other, even though you strike the keys; a wedge of felt or rubber will serve as a mute. At first it is wise to proceed cautiously, making one adjustment at a time and testing the results by playing familiar pieces of music containing the note concerned, for it takes time to become accustomed to the relative abstraction in the sound of two or three unison strings or a simple octave interval by itself. Make absolutely certain that you have one note (i.e. all two or three strings) right before you proceed to another,

or you will undermine the whole tuning of the instrument. At this stage, do the best you can in tuning the instrument 'to itself'. To tune a note to a tuning fork or other standard is almost certain to mean that the whole piano has to be retuned.

For the most difficult and important part, laying the bearing, there is really no substitute for judgment of beats, and this cannot be acquired quickly or on a piano which you hope to use meanwhile. On a piano which is badly out of tune and virtually unplayable, a reasonable temperament can however be established on the basis of a one-octave chromatic pitch-pipe (a mouth-organ of concert pitch which is fairly cheap and will give the pitch of twelve notes in the central area), although here great accuracy is needed in matching the string to the note of the pipe with its reed-tone. A set of twelve tuning forks is another, much more expensive, means to the same end. There are various electronic signal generators producing audible and accurate pitches throughout the piano's range. More useful, but still more costly, is such a generator (whose note may not be audible) with a visual beat-meter to indicate whether a struck string is sharp or flat in relation to the generated pitch.

A word of caution is needed about the use of expensive accessories which cover most of the compass of a piano. They are valuable aids, but they will not tune a piano for you and their usefulness in fact increases with experience. It must be remembered that these devices are mathematical in basis. As you go up a piano, probably in part because of the stiffness of the strings the octave harmonic rises increasingly above the pitch which would be strictly appropriate to the note an octave above the starting-point. The tuner hears this and tunes somewhat sharp ('stretching the octaves') because of it. As he goes by ear, he has little choice, and this rather than any tendency of the upper regions to go flat sooner, is the reason for sharpness towards the top and is essential if the piano is to sound fully in tune. There is no set rule—it depends on the individual instrument. If you use your equipment and not your ear you may end up with a passable tuning, for your purposes and depending on the piano, but it is likely to seem rather dead and toneless because you have failed to make these adjustments to the harmonics. Some electronic tuners help you towards a solution by permitting you to register clearly on them the second harmonic as well as the fundamental pitch and to tune accordingly. On the whole, however, it is wiser and, eventually, quicker, to use these accessories as guides mainly for the middle range (which in any case they show most clearly) and to tune the rest as far as possible by heard octaves (checking with octaves two or three apart, with common chords and other intervals).

However you go about a complete tuning rather than a touching up of excruciating unisons, the results at first are likely to be somewhat dispiriting. It is better initially to put off this objective and to concentrate on developing your ear by tuning unisons and octaves in the middle area. For example, select the string which is currently tuned to best fit with the octave below or above and tune the other strings into perfect unison (a quiet, single sound) with it. You will find that such dodges as plucking single strings and holding sounds on the sustaining pedal are useful at this stage. Initially, the needs are to learn to listen (especially as the sound dies away after striking) and to be familiar with the feel of strings and tuning hammer (lever) at various points of the piano's compass. When you have some idea of the latter, you can extend to the lower bichords and upper trichords, noting the great difference of movement required to produce a small change of pitch in either

register. For a while, leave the bass monochords, whose fundamental pitches can be difficult to distinguish, and the very top notes where the movements required are very small.

Opinions differ on the best type of tuning hammer. Some prefer a T shape as giving direct pressure of the pins into the holes, and this certainly is beneficial with grand pianos, whilst others prefer the leverage of an offset handle. The star type of socket is of most use, since it allows of more positions on the pin, but beware that modern hammers do not always fit nineteenth century pins, and a special purchase, or improvisation with a small socket spanner, may be needed.

You will notice that there is spring, apparently in the hammer but in fact also in the tuning pins, and it is here that the skill of setting lies, together with distributing the tension throughout the strings, for it is no use having the strings in pitch if they are out again next day. Particularly with the topmost strings you have to allow for the spring and tighten very slightly beyond the required tension and, if you are flattening, you will go slightly further than intended until you are used to the effect. In the treble of a well-pinned piano you may indeed make adjustments of pitch without being aware that the pin has moved in its hole at all, but merely that you have applied pressure on the lever.

Broken strings are very rare occurrences and they are not necessarily disastrous (see Chapter 6, 'Note not sounding'). They are caused primarily by wrenching on a string when listening to another, and by pulling too hard on the correct string when it has become set in its agraffe or around the pin through lack of tuning. Neglected, rusty strings in an old piano are inevitably at risk, but it is often possible to repair them. Care will avoid many breakages—make a habit of letting a string off lightly before you increase its tension, and at the same time pluck this string to make sure that you have identified it. Try to 'set' a string downwards— go very slightly above required pitch and gradually come down, striking the key firmly as you do so. This will help the string to stay in tune over a period—it is one thing to tune a piano and another to get it to stay in tune.

The inexperienced are likely to find a continuous mute more nuisance than it is worth. If you cannot buy proper tuning mutes (i.e. felt or rubber wedges) pieces of pointed rubber can be satisfactory, and you will probably devise your own methods of using them. With trichords you have of course to blank off two strings for separate tuning, but the third can be adjusted to the unison already tuned. Uprights are difficult to mute in the upper register where the dampers and hammers obstruct access for the wedges. It is possible to proceed after a fashion by plucking individual strings, but the best answer is a pair of scissor-mutes (known as Papp mutes) (Fig. 20), which are long and thin enough to pass over the hammer rail and between the hammer shanks.

Fig. 20 Papp mutes for tuning upright pianos

Using these methods, you will be able to remove a discord due to a poor unison or octave and to make other improvements to an instrument seriously out of tune. You will not for a while be able to satisfy yourself that you can tune a piano, and eventually you will be determined to lay your own bearing from the single note of a tuning fork. Meanwhile, however, you will have acquired a great deal of practical knowledge, been able to make a discordant piano more or less acceptable, and will have acquired a sensitivity to pitch which you did not have before. If you are then more positive and exact in discussion with your piano tuner, so much the better; but do not, unless you have good reasons to doubt him, decide that you know as much as he does about the job and could do it if you had the time. You could—but the time is years, not hours.

Toning (Voicing)

This is the adjustment of a piano's tone quality by working on its hammers. Nothing in connection with pianos is apparently more simple and nothing is in fact more difficult or dependent on experience. Mistakes here are more likely to be calamitous than errors in tuning or regulating or even in stringing, for they are very difficult to correct.

The hammer felts can be filed with sandpaper, pricked with needles of various sizes, or pressed with a hot iron or in pliers. Ironing may be needed for the highest hammers when the felt is brand new. Otherwise, the resort to ironing is a desperate one. The tone given out by felt properly tense on the outside but compressed within is far fuller and brighter than the thud of felts which have been pressed with an iron, generally because the process of softening has been taken too far. Needle-holders can be bought from suppliers and hold two or three needles at a time. Slower but satisfactory work can be done with a single needle in a pin-chuck bought from a tool shop. In principle, if the tone is hard, the felt can be softened by pricking it (Fig. 21). If the tone is offensive

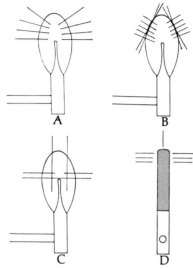

Fig. 21 Some methods of toning
A Deep toning
B Shallow toning
C Exceptionally deep toning
D How *NOT* to insert the needles

when the piano is played loudly, the inside of the hammer is too compressed, and a fine needle has to be pushed into it fairly deeply towards the back of the shoulder. If the tone at low dynamic is hard, a somewhat finer needle is used, still as a rule radially, but rather nearer to the striking surface. Taking 'stitches' of greater or lesser depth is also possible here. Mere teasing on the surface does

not last, but shallow toning, although it will need repeating periodically, is often necessary for a good tone at low volume. One has to be very wary of touching the point of impact itself, for very slight work here will produce drastic results and break down the felt irretrievably. The very hard felts often found in old pianos can also be softened throughout by sending fine needles up through the top and bottom of the hammer, with the length of the hammer (never across it), towards the striking surface. This is the deepest and most drastic way of toning. It is risky and surprisingly hard work. There are in fact many ways of toning, and only experience will tell you in advance which may be best for a particular condition. Experience also is necessary for you to feel the density of the felt and the quality of the sound given out.

The owner must be most careful in this area, though perhaps it is the most tempting for improvement. If he is not, he will produce no improvement but rather land himself with the necessity of having all the hammers refelted—and perhaps also of finding a new tuner. It is prudent to concentrate on a few notes whose tone is plainly anomalous when compared with that of their neighbours, having first made certain that the difference is not due to tuning, for adjusting the whole scale of tone throughout a piano is a much more difficult undertaking. Even then, care should be taken to decide at the outset what are the notes beyond which one will not venture and to stick to that decision; it is so easy when toning to soften one hammer a little, then a little more, then its neighbour, then back to the first, and so on. The result is a dead piano. The same is true of filing out trenches in hammers (see Chapter 6, 'The "Old Joanna" sound'), where particularly as little should be done to the actual striking point as possible. The impulse of the novice voicer is to beautify by softening, but so often it is not so much softening as new strings or accurate tuning which would beautify the sound. To soften the felts is to reduce the vibrations of partials, and these vibrations, in due proportions, are necessary for there to be fullness and life in the tone.

Over-filing and over-needling can be compensated for by ironing. For this use an iron—ideally a flat bar such as an old chisel heated, but a household iron will do—heated till it will just scorch the felt. Start below each shoulder, top and bottom, and press the felt up towards the striking point. Subsequently go over the surfaces very lightly with a sand-paper file to remove any charred felt or excessive discolouration. This will harden the felts, and indeed some light needling will be needed in places afterwards, but the tone will never be what it should be, for the tension of the felt as it bends round the head has been teased out by the needle, and the heavy compaction produced by ironing has been substituted.

It is often held that toning is a craft to be reserved for the practised tuner or technician of many years' experience. There is much to be said for the view; but it is inevitable that the discovery that one's tuner is not well qualified in this area is often made too late, when the damage is done. In this connection it is interesting to note the very practical remarks of Alfred Brendel in his *Thoughts and Afterthoughts* (1976). Most of us cannot aspire to be pianists of the calibre of Brendel, but many a pianist will be driven, by the sheer difficulty of getting the job done to his satisfaction by someone else, to attempt some voicing himself; and, provided he is always cautious and allows himself time and playing in which to weigh up the effects of each adjustment, he should achieve considerable improvement in the sound of his instrument.

6 Faults and adjustments

In this chapter are listed some of the commonest faults in pianos, particularly old and inadequately serviced pianos. In many cases the owner himself can produce improvement, though he will have to decide according to his own ability, experience and the risk involved whether this should be left to a technician. It should be noted that to regulate a grand action, the action has to be removed from the case (see Chapter 3, 'Access within'). With uprights some adjustments can be made with the action in place. On the overall requirements in regulating actions, see Chapter 4, 'The action'.

The order of this list of defects is somewhat random, but is generally according to the seriousness of the fault from the point of view of the player. In fact, of course, defects seldom come singly, and many of them overlap. Fuller treatment of some matters will be found elsewhere in the book, for which the Index should be consulted. Faults in fine tuning are omitted as being not easily defined and best left to be dealt with by the tuner (whether or not the owner) in the light of experience.

Touch

Key sticks up

First, the key front may have jumped too high and lodged on top of the oval pin at the front. In this case it cannot be depressed at all. After removing the fall and key-retaining slip (on a grand), remove the key and replace it correctly, turning the oval pin to engage with the front key bushing very slightly, and fluffing-up or replacing this bushing if necessary. The grand's slip should be set with 2mm clearance over the keys at rest. Save in the case of the grand, where the slip may be too high, this trouble is produced by rough handling rather than a fault in the action. If the oval pin is short in comparison with its neighbours, it can be raised by unscrewing it and, if necessary, plugging its hole in the keyframe. Of course a paper-clip or other obstacle may lodge under a key, and a sticking key may also be caused by any form of solid jamming in the action itself.

Much commoner is the key which sticks on the way up and can be depressed only with noise and difficulty. The trouble is likely to be rubbing of neighbouring keys or too tight an oval pin and bushing. Rubbing of adjacent keys may be due to a loose piece of foreign matter or to warping or swelling of the wood of any of the keys. A badly warped key can be cured by appropriate clamping and repeated steaming (which for a while will swell the wood) but generally treating with medium sandpaper will be sufficient. The oval pin should be turned and the bush adjusted so that the key has perceptible freedom laterally, but no more. Bushes can be loosened by squeezing in long-nosed pliers or, more drastically, dampening and then steaming under pressure from a hot soldering iron. Do not be too severe on this if the piano is new to you—the cause may have been a dampness which in new surroundings will cure itself, when the bush is likely to be loose rather than tight. Where a bush is worn through by rubbing on the pin (whether the oval or the balance pin) it is fairly easily replaced with similar cloth or thin felt, although in the centre this may entail removing the chase with a hot knife. Rusted pins, oval or centre, cause noise and rubbing. Steel wool and fine abrasive paper will cure the trouble. A flick of graphite powder may help further.

Key sticks down or returns slowly

Slow return may be due to some obstruction as mentioned above, but it has other causes and the diagnosis depends on whether the key is naturally balanced to drop forward when free of the action. If the weight of the action holds the keybacks down, the forward-balanced key will stay forward if the action jams up, so attention will have to shift to stiffness in the action if the key can be raised freely by hand. Of course the action may also be jammed if a back-balanced key stays down, but then the key is more likely being held by some friction on itself. The freedom of the action can be tested readily enough by moving the front of the wippen. A sluggish but freely moving key is likely to be due to a broken damper- or hammer-spring or, though this is not usually the sole factor, to too slack a bridle tape.

These points (save for damper-spring and tape) apply equally to grands. Their keys are of course balanced forwards to counteract the weight of the hammers. The weight of the action, even without the hammer, will normally ensure a fairly swift return. Sluggishness and even actual sticking are more likely to be due to friction or obstruction in the keyboard than to a staying-up of the action due merely to neglect or disrepair.

Heavy or irregular touch

For general regulation of touch, see Chapter 4, 'The action'. It has been mentioned that touch is a compound of several factors, notably the key's inertia, the weight of the hammer, and the timing of raising the damper and of escapement. Heavy touch, beyond what is consistent and inherent in the inertia, is produced most often by stiff (possibly replaced or bent) damper springs in an upright, and by raising the dampers before key and hammer have gained momentum. With a suspect note, check that the damper moves well before escapement occurs and when the hammer is about half-way to the string (tantamount to some 3mm of key-dip). If it moves too early, take out the action and bend the offending damper spoon inward (i.e. away from the strings), say a couple of millimetres, experimenting until there is an improvement. (A tool for bending damper spoons with the action in place can be had from suppliers.) Observe whether the damper spring differs from its neighbours and either ease it by bending or replace it if necessary. It is a mistake to try to compensate for poor damper felts by stiffening the springs, for the change is apparent in the touch.

The touch will again seem heavy if (in an upright) the hammer of the note concerned is seen to be raised from the hammer rail when the key is at rest. Adjust it by lowering the capstan screw at the end of the key where it meets the wippen foot, taking this to the point where the hammer is squarely on the rail but there is virtually no free movement of the key. It may also be that escapement is occurring early and so coinciding, as it should not, with a correctly set damper. If the hammer falls back, when the key is pressed fairly slowly, before it is within 2–3mm of the string, raise the let-off escapement button by turning its looped wire, or flattened stub-head anti-clockwise. A slotted screwdriver or metal rod is best for this. Keep raising the button in this way until the hammer comes as close as it can to the string without ever sticking or bouncing there. In an old action, this distance may be somewhat larger than 2mm.

Everything in the previous sections (on sticking keys) applies here also to grands as well as uprights. In a grand, however, heavy touch is usually caused by stiffness in the action, by a sticking damper (which will also return slowly and cause lingering sound), or by a damper engaging too early. Sticking can sometimes be cured by wobbling the damper. More often, the action has to be removed. Check that the damper lever is no lower than those adjacent, raising it by the grub-screw if it is lower—if the damper engages late with the damper lever correctly set level, adjustment will have to be made to the end of the key by adding felt. Take the damper out from above after undoing the grubscrew, then clean the wire with steel wool or a wire brush. It may be worth rubbing the wire with graphite powder (or a soft pencil) to lubricate it. Return the wire, set the lever correctly on it and test for freedom. If the damper still sticks, remove the damper again, heat the wire and rub it up and down in the bushing. Only as a last resort gently turn a broach in the bushing to enlarge it. Remember that damper troubles on grands tend to be rather seasonal, and you do not want the wire to be sloppy when the bushing opens out again. It is as well while doing this job to check the freedom of the damper lever centre. If it is tight, treat it with graphite; or a drop of water which will swell the surrounding wood after which it will recede over a period; or, extremely, by driving out the pin with a punch and slightly opening the flange bushings. (See also below, 'Action noisy'.) This will involve removing the whole lever rail and all the levers, but the lever rail is simply screwed on each side and should present no problems.

The hammer and wippen centres may also come under suspicion if the action is sluggish, and these are treated as the damper lever centre.

There are certain simple causes of jamming or hesitant action (and also of disturbing noises) which are easily overlooked. These include the rubbing of the hammer head against its check as the head rises (bend the check out as little as necessary) in a grand and, in uprights, the rubbing of adjacent bridle wires, tapes and checks, where again the cure is to bend the offending wires.

All these points at least should be checked before it is decided to alter the balance of any keys. Changing the poise will have little effect if there is trouble elsewhere and will be contrary to the design. In an extreme case, it is however possible to remove or add lead to a key. Keys are very brittle and must be well drilled before lead or sections of nails are tapped into them.

See also 'Heavy touch when soft pedal used', below.

Light or irregular touch
The first thing to check is the condition of the key bushings. Slack at the front end should be taken up by turning the oval pin, and the bushings may need to be fluffed up with a needle or totally replaced.

Hammer weights must be presumed to be those of a manufacturer for the action and should not be altered. A common 'repair' of a broken treble hammer is, however, to replace it with the hammer of the top note, since the latter is less often used. This produces light touch and poor tone in the lower note, depending on its distance from the top. If the old head is in the case, as may well be, it should be reshanked with straight-grained dowel and glued into place, taking great care as to the exact length and to the angle of the head. If the head or butt is missing there is nothing that can be done at all simply without access to specialist supplies, though it is possible to cut and file up a new head from hardwood and fit hard felt. (See also below, 'Note not sounding—total'.)

Broken, incorrect or merely slack damper springs produce light touch and so, but with a special sensation, does improper adjustment of the action to the keys of an upright. If the jack starts well below the hammer butt, the key will move for part of its journey doing nothing, however heavy it may appear later. This is rectified by upward adjustment of the capstan screw at the back of the key, leaving only a thin card's thickness between jack and butt. Broken hammer springs also slightly affect touch.

Light touch in a grand may be caused by the use of a substitute hammer head, as above, but is usually due to extensive wear, particularly in the key bushings. In a really worn instrument, the jacks may not fully engage with the hammer rollers (where their tips should align with the wooden splints in the middle of the rollers). The rollers have then to be made good with soft leather and the jack stop screw and spring to be adjusted. The repetition lever and spring may also need adjustment so that the jack is just free beneath the roller when the action is at rest.

Where a grand's touch is initially free and then resistance is felt, provided it is a model with normal repetition action, the hammers are likely to be found lying on their rests, rather than with their weight supported by the repetition levers, and the strike distance will exceed 50mm. Turn up the key capstans until the strike distance is correct—on no account lift the hammers by raising the repetition levers, or the jacks will engage late. It is simplest to get the two outer hammers to 50mm, then to remove the action and to set the others by means of a gauge or string between the two hammers already set. The adjustment of old non-repetition actions, where the hammer shanks *should* rest on the rail, is similar to that of uprights.

Repetition

'Repetition' refers to the facility for rapidly repeating a single note. In practice it is more important than the name might suggest, since of course it extends in some degree to all rapid playing.

The upright is not given to quick repetition, since even in modern actions the hammers must return virtually to rest and the keys to level before the jacks will again relocate under their hammer butts. Moreover, the damper springing imparts an unfavourable touch. Nonetheless, the action can be adjusted to its best, and this is by means of hammer spring, check and bridle tape. Many an old upright has broken or missing hammer springs, whether mounted on a rail or of the now general type where the spring is fixed in the butt and engages with a silk loop glued to the flange. An action will function without hammer springs, but not well. All these springs are readily replaced from springy steel wire of appropriate gauge, and new loops of nylon or thread can be glued to the flanges as necessary. The check should be adjusted by bending its wire until the hammer bounces back against it at about 20mm, or a bit less than half the strike distance. Felt on both hammer stop and check can be replaced. Whilst a level line of checks looks well, it cannot always be achieved with a worn action, and it is more important that the check is well positioned for each hammer.

The contribution of the tape to uprights varies, but usually it substantially aids rapid return of the hammer on release of the key. It is slack and looped whilst the jack is driving, but comes suddenly taut as the key and wippen move away in advance of the hammer. It can only be adjusted (by bending the bridle wire and fitting new tips of thin leather) with the action in place. With the key capstan set at a height to give the jack very slight lost motion against the butt, the tape should be set straight but not actually tight: the capstan, not the tape, should be taking the weight of the wippen. Broken tapes must be repaired since the further function of the tapes is to keep the jacks and wippens in place when the action is removed. Without them, there is the great inconvenience of having to lift the jacks back into place individually as one struggles to mount the action. This is a sure way to cause damage.

Lack of clearance between jack and hammer butt is a common cause of poor repetition in uprights (see 'Heavy or irregular touch' above), since it results in unreliable relocation of the jack after playing a note. This is the usual cause of the mysterious note which plays once but not twice. A weak or missing jack spring will also contribute to the trouble.

As we have seen, repetition is a cardinal virtue of the grand action as now generally built. The repetition lever is sprung to hold the hammer at such a height that the jack can slip underneath the hammer roller to deliver a fresh, though less powerful, blow when the key has not been returned fully to level, Regulation is no easy matter and depends on the relative strengths of springs as well as on the setting of screws and checks. When escapement occurs and the jack flies free of the hammer roller, the hammer falls back initially as far as is permitted by the repetition lever, which is governed by the hammer shank flange regulating screw at the top of the action. This 'drop' should be about 2mm. Given a harder blow, the hammer will bounce back, compressing the spring of the lever, until it is caught by the check. This is set, as in the upright, so that it arrests the hammer when it is some 20mm from the string—and also so that the hammer head does not touch it on the way to the string, but only on returning. If the key is then slightly released, the jack is no longer caught by the regulating button, and the hammer comes free of the check. Provided that the lever's spring is not too strong, the repetition lever then raises the hammer, without permitting it to bounce onto the string, into a position where the jack relocates under the roller and the note can be struck again, although the key has not been fully released. If the lever's spring is too strong, the hammer bounces, and if it is too weak the hammer does not properly return and the action is sluggish. The way of adjusting the strength of the lever's spring varies according to model, but should be plain from observation. It must also be ensured that the checks really do hold the hammers. The head backs may need roughening with a coarse file or fine saw-cuts to bring this about, for they wear smooth. There is one simple caution in striking grand keys with the action out of the case; do not strike them so hard that the hammers rise beyond vertical or there is a great risk of breaking hammer shanks.

Heavy touch when soft pedal is used
As was mentioned in Chapter 1, this is a feature of upright pianos and is due to the lack of time between the taking up of the hammers' weight and the raising of the dampers. Unless the dampers are ill-set (see 'Heavy or irregular touch' above), they are best not altered. It is preferable to make the engagement of the hammers slightly earlier, somewhat lessening the effect of the soft pedal—a choice of evils. The adjustment is primarily by slackening the tensioning screw attached to the pedal itself. If this results in too slack a feeling to the pedal, it is possible to bend the crank arm on the movable part of the hammer rail so that the connecting rod meets it later, or to remove some felt from the rod. Means of adjustment vary according to make but should be self-evident.

In an elderly piano it should also be checked that escapement is occurring as near to the string as possible since, apart from other considerations, it is desirable that the resistances of hammer weight, dampers and escapement be spread through the keys' descent.

Sound

Note not sounding—total
It is assumed that the key moves freely up and down—otherwise, see 'Touch' above.

The immediately obvious causes are a broken or missing string or a missing hammer head. The latter is common in old pianos exposed to central heating, where dry heat causes the shanks to become brittle. Broken hammer shanks can be wound with thread or fine twine and glued. New shanks of hard, straight-grained dowel can be made, but remember that the quality of the shank considerably affects the rebound of hammer from string, and so the tone; any old stick will not do. Metal pins and splints should be avoided as impairing tone. A new head may be acquired from a secondhand piano dealer, or switched, in the classic execrable repair, from elsewhere in the piano. It is also possible to make up a head from hardwood, but this is a long job. If a switched head is too small, it will be unsightly and light. Do not try to increase its bulk by adding a layer of felt—a great part of the tone derives from the tension of the felt, and a fairly thin layer round an existing circle cannot have that tension and will be spongy and toneless. If you can recover the substituted head with hard felt to the right thickness, that will be better, but will still not be equivalent to the correct proportions of wood and felt. (See 'The "Old Joanna" sound' below.)

A similar trouble found in older pianos, especially if they are roughly handled, is a jack with the heel snapped off. As a result, the jack never engages or never escapes. A replacement piece is not difficult to file to shape and glue into place.

The strings which are most likely to break are wound bass strings, but they usually break in the unwound ends. As a result they can be repaired by, if necessary, stripping back the winding, and then forming of the end, and of new wire of the same gauge, loops which are pushed into each other to form a reef knot (Fig. 22). This is not as easy as it appears, owing to the resistance of the wire, but patience will eventually be rewarded. Such a string will sound quite reasonable even if the break is in its speaking length, but it will need several tunings before it will hold pitch.

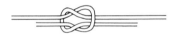

Fig. 22 Knotting a string

You may be able to obtain an adequate, if not identical, string from a piano dealer. New wound strings can as a rule be obtained only through tuners and others with access to specialist suppliers who tend to deal exclusively with professionals.

Plain wire strings break less often and it may be said that strings of any sort break rarely if they are sensibly tuned. They are replaceable from spring steel piano wire of appropriate gauge, which can be had from good hardware shops. If you have to replace a string, first take off the pressure bar if there is one. In some cases it is simplest for access to remove the two tuning pins involved, although, if you can extract the old string merely by loosening them two or three turns and will be able to fit the new string, so much the better. (Tuning pins are screwed out, but should be driven straight in with a hammer and a stout punch.) Cut new wire by reference to the old, or allowing 65mm spare beyond each pin, and bend the wire first in the right place for the hitchpin. In what follows, try not to kink the wire, for this can spoil its tone. Drive in the pins, if they were removed, till the threads just cease to show, and wind three turns of wire closely onto one, keeping the wire under tension by hand. Take the wire through any agraffe before winding onto the pin, then go on to the bridge, round the hitchpin, back over the bridge, through the next agraffe (if any), and through the second pin, onto which it is similarly wound. Have the wire taut enough to stay in place and check its location between the bridge pins and at the base of the hitchpin, then tighten it, but not to pitch, and drive the pins in. The coils should be straightened with a lever (Fig. 23) so that they are close together and there is no more than 1–2mm space between the lowest coil and the wrestplank or frame (which the wire must not touch). Do not drive the pins in further, for there is a risk that the plank will split. Replace the pressure bar and space the strings regularly before bringing the string up to pitch. The area of work is likely to be wildly, and much of the instrument slightly, out of tune, and the new string will need to be tuned five or six times before it will hold pitch.

Full restringing is similar. It is best to start with the overstrung section and then to loosen alternate strings before removing them all. This ensures that there is no sudden damaging reduction of tension in the frame. The dampers of a grand should be removed when restringing, despite the time which removal takes, or they are very likely to be broken. Lay them out or hang them in order, or number them. With an upright it is almost essential to remove the whole keybed for access. It is possible to slacken strings, cut them and then wind them off pins, leaving the pins in, but it is worthwhile taking all the pins out and inspecting the condition of the wrestplank at the same time as restringing. When you have all the strings off, it makes sense to check and clean the soundboard, and to attend to any loose pins on the bridges (see 'Notes rattle, whistle or ring', below). Restringing, using the same wire

Fig. 23 Coil-straightening lever of bent steel strip
A Leather backing on heel to protect frame

gauges and replacing worn felts, is largely a matter of common sense, and not in itself very expensive (if wound strings are cleaned rather than replaced), but it is a large undertaking and hard on the hands. It is also an opportunity to replace or tighten tuning pins (see 'Piano will not stay in tune' below) for, since five or six tunings will be needed initially, loose pins are a complication one can do without.

The other major cause of a free key but no sound is total failure of the jack to drive the hammer. This may be through very bad adjustment, through faults concerned with repetition (see 'Repetition' above), or because of stiff jack centres and weak jack springs. The adjustment is that of the key capstan in uprights; if it is screwed too high, the jack locates imperfectly if at all under the hammer butt. The same trouble occurs in grands if a jack regulating (stop) screw is so far advanced that the jack cannot meet the hammer roller; the tip of the jack should align with the front of the wooden splint in the middle of the roller when the action is at rest. A stiff centre may be loosened with a drop of water on the wood and left over a period, or by punching out the pin and very lightly opening the flange bushings—this is best done with a hot wire or needle, for cutting the cloth will roughen it and make things worse. Graphite powder also may help. Jack springs may be stretched to tighten them. They should be sufficient to hold the jacks right up against gravity when the wippens are held with spoons upwards, but not make more than the lightest click when allowed to spring up in this way. Jack springs on grands vary in design, but are not subject to the same weakening from compression as are those of uprights.

Note not sounding with normal touch
This is that most irritating fault when one has to remember in playing that a note requires an extra heavy touch if it is to provide the same volume as its neighbours. The symptom is really one of defective touch (see 'Heavy or irregular touch') or repetition (see 'Repetition' above). If the note will sound, but only with heavier

touch, a common cause is when an upright's damper is too far advanced and the spring's resistance is encountered when the key is hardly depressed, or when it is retarded and escapement and raising of the damper coincide. A stiff hammer or wippen centre, or minor obstruction such as a broken hammer spring fallen into the works can also cause the trouble. Where the note will not sound at all after having just previously sounded, the trouble lies in repetition and, in the upright, usually the capstan is set too high so that the jack cannot relocate.

Wrong note or several notes played by one key
These faults are generally produced by inaccurate alignment of hammers and strings or, especially with the old raised capstans, by bent capstans (or warped keys) which raise more than one wippen when a key is depressed. The cure for the latter is obviously to straighten the capstan and key and to rebush the key if necessary (see 'Key sticks up' above). Sometimes hammer flanges are worn or have play and can be screwed back in the proper position, if necessary with a paper washer to raise one side. Warped shanks can be carefully straightened in steam from a kettle or replaced. A loose head is best removed (for which heat will be needed, though alternatively it can be broken off and the shank hole drilled clean) and reglued in proper alignment. The course of strings with agraffes cannot be altered, but strings under pressure bars can be moved after loosening the bar. A gauge of stout metal with slots for the strings is useful in obtaining regular spacing with a pressure bar. Retuning will then be needed. In grands, two notes at once can be sounded if the stop screw (normally fitted in the right hand keyblock) to the action shift is missing or not set. The action can then travel too far when the soft pedal is used.

Notes sound 'bonk' or 'bim-bam'

This is a crude description of defects known as 'bounce' and 'blocking', the former of which can be hard to eliminate in some actions. In effect, the hammer either hits the string and remains pressed against it, or hits it twice, so that the second stroke sounds like an echo or smudging of the note. The causes are usually failure or partial failure of escapement, or too high a setting or strong a spring with the grand's repetition lever, together with weak checking. 'Bonk' is of course also produced by a damper which fails to rise.

If the jack fails to escape, the escapement let-off button in grand or upright requires to be screwed down. As has been said, the closer the hammer can come to the string before the jack is forced to release, the better, but not to the extent that there is a risk that escapement will not occur at all, and a larger distance may have to be adopted to avoid all risk of 'bonk'. In old ill-maintained pianos the fault is common, for the let-off button felt wears thin and the button may indeed fall off, in which case escapement cannot occur. (In due course, if the hammers are very worn or have been extensively filed, there will be no room to take up lost motion by screwing up the escapement button further. Then the hammers will have to be recovered or, as a stop-gap measure, the felt on the button can be reduced.)

'Bounce' may occur in uprights if escapement is left too late, checking is poor, a tape is very loose or the hammer spring is weak or missing, but it is primarily a failing of grands. The repetition lever has to be of sufficient strength to cushion the hammer in its descent to the check, and to return it to repetition height (see 'Repetition' above), but if it is too strong and the lever rises too high and too fast, bounce will result. A compromise has to be found. It cannot be found unless the checking is adequate to hold the hammer against the repetition lever spring's pull when the key is down. The leather or felt of the check may have to be renewed, and the back of the hammer head should be roughened with a coarse file or with fine saw cuts. The check should hold the hammer head some 20mm from the string and must be so placed that it cannot touch the latter as it rises when the key is first depressed. The check can be tightened by screwing it in if its wire is at all loose.

Staccato impossible or poor

Good as is modern damping, it may be said that few pianos are completely silent when the keys are released after the playing of a big chord. The cut-off depends partly on the design and material of the damper felts, considerably on their adjustment, and partly on resonance within the instrument itself. About the latter little can be done. It may be noted also that uprights' dampers are generally less efficient, in part because they move in an arc, than those of grands.

Regulation of dampers has been mentioned above as it affects touch (see 'Heavy touch', 'Light touch'). We must ensure that dampers rest solidly on the strings when all pressure is removed from the keys, and neither stop high nor rub against each other. The test can be aural or by pushing the strings backwards (downwards in grands) to ensure that dampers follow. The angle of the felt to the string is critical in uprights and can be adjusted both by loosening and moving the heads and by bending the wires slightly with a notched screwdriver head or rod for access. The flat heads should not be glued rigidly to the wood through which the wires pass; slackness here (they are usually mounted on felt) permits some self-adjustment of damper to string. The angles of grands' dampers can often be adjusted by gentle wobbling of their wires; at the worst, the action must be removed and the wire loosened and turned in relation to the damper lever.

Whether in grands or uprights, there must be clearance from the sustaining pedal mechanism. Thus there should be some play in the pedal before it raises the dampers (see above, Chapter 3, 'The Pedals'). In a grand the damper levers must be in a straight line or the sustaining action will be irregular. Therefore provided the damper heads are level, early or late damping of single notes is best corrected by attending to the felt at the key tips rather than by adjusting the damper wires, which will leave damper levers high or low in relation to their neighbours.

Uprights' damper springs can be renewed without difficulty with spring steel wire—the springs tend to stay in place ineffectively although in fact broken half-way through. The free end of a spring causes noise if it does not lie on a piece of soft felt, which may need replacement. Freeing dampers in grands is described above (see 'Heavy touch'). Adding weights to the damper levers will affect touch and is an admission of failure.

Occasionally problems are found, particularly if an action has been removed, in uprights at notes close to frame bars. This is caused by rubbing of damper or wippen on the bar and, provided the action is well-placed, can be cured by sanding down the affected part. The defect is usually evident from marks on the bars' paintwork.

Damper felts can sometimes be renewed with substitutes, such as chiropody felt, if correct felt is not obtainable. Old felts may also be improved by teazing with a needle.

The sticking or 'missing' of a damper should be distinguished from a tendency for the sound of notes, fairly generally, to linger and mingle with the notes struck immediately next, thus producing a blurred and discordant effect. This is caused by premature raising (and so also late falling) of dampers by the keys (in a grand) or wippens (in an upright), and may occur even though the dampers in fact damp properly when they are on the strings. In this event the damping may sound acceptable for single notes, though the touch may feel heavy, but not in course of playing a passage. There are of course degrees of the fault. The only remedy is to remove the action, bend the damper spoons back (in an upright), or loosen the grubscrews on the damper levers (in a grand) and slightly lower the damper wires in the levers (Fig. 24). In the end, levers and spoons should be in a reasonably straight line and the dampers should not move until the keys are depressed some 3mm. Levers are 3–4mm above key tails in the grand. It is worth taking trouble with this adjustment, as it can lead to a cleaner sound and lighter touch.

Notes rattle, whistle or ring

Apart from noises in the keys (see 'Touch' above), there are unwanted sounds from the strings which can be difficult to track down. Before trying to trace them the instrument must be in tune, for they are not always distinguishable readily from defective unisons.

The chief sources of trouble are wound strings and bridge pins. The windings of bass and tenor strings become filled with dirt and can be cleaned by soaking in petrol or paraffin and brushing with a wire brush, preferably motorised. Badly encrusted strings can be lightly sanded first. This will also brighten their appearance. If a coil is unwinding at the end it can be soft-soldered into place, using a minimum of solder. With elderly strings the best course is to place the eye over the hitchpin and then to twist the string on its axis (in the direction of the winding) once or even twice before fastening at the wrestpin. The twisting tightens the winding round the core and improves vibrancy. Ensure that the twisted eye is so placed that the wire end presses into the frame, preventing movement and is not sticking up free.

If a bridge pin is pulled backwards by a string it tears the bridge and remains loose, with the further result that two pins can be so close that a string is caught between them. This results in a poor tone and sometimes a noise like a whistle or ringing sound. Isolated instances can be cured by loosening the strings concerned and tapping their pins home. This has generally to be at their new and less satisfactory angle, since they are too short to bed firmly at the proper angle and will be liable to tear the bridge further. The soundboard should be supported as far as possible from behind if you are hammering on the bridge or you will have a loose bridge or cracked soundboard to add to your troubles.

When damage to the top of the bridge is widespread it may be possible to remove the bridge and to plane the top surface down. First measure the height of the bridge exactly and, in an old piano, allow an extra millimetre for lost down bearing. When planing, leave the pin holes visible and deepen the cut-outs at the edges of the bridge. Drill to about two-thirds of the new pins' length before knocking them in. If no adjustment is made to height, the bridge will then be rather low and will need moving slightly towards the treble. Provided that the strings will press down onto the bridge, the height may be dispensed with, but it is risky, and failure will not be detected until too late when the piano has been reassembled. It is preferable, therefore, to pack the bridge with

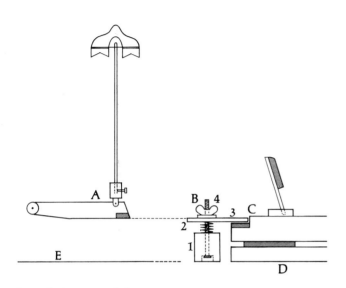

Fig. 24 Regulating grand dampers
A Damper lever and adjustable wire
B Improvised tool for relating height of key tail to damper lever
C Key tail
D Keyframe, on table or firm surface with B
E Keybed, on which B, when set from key tail, is placed as gauge for damper lever height
1 Wooden block about 8cms long and 2.5cms high
2 Compression spring adjusted to hold slip level
3 Wooden or hardboard slip 3–4mm thick and about 2.5cms long. (The thickness is critical and determines the regulation)
4 Bolt, wing-nut and washer

Maintenance

12 **Inside a grand piano** (above) Regulating buttons and capstans visible
with fall (lid) removed
Inside a grand piano (below) Damper levers and wires visible with
action and keyboard removed; note connecting rod and sustaining and
soft pedals

13 **Inside a grand piano** Detail of agraffes (studs), dampers and damper levers seen from above

137152

resin or wood moulded to the curve of the soundboard below. If this is not practicable, and long enough pins are fitted, it is also possible to pack the top of the bridge with glued veneer to increase downbearing.

The bridge must be perfectly fitted, glued and preferably dowelled, into place on the soundboard using the old screw or dowel holes as guides. It is simplest to remove old dowels, glue and temporarily screw the bridge into position and, when the glue has set, to remove the screws, drill out the holes and insert new dowels in their place. In a further effort to restore downbearing, wooden edges to the hitchpin plate may be able to be lowered and the thickness of the felt at this bearing may stand reduction. Such repairs are likely to affect tone, but not necessarily for the worse, and are practical rather than commendable on an old instrument. Strictly, a new beech top or cap is fitted to the bridge and pinned, but this is work for the experienced restorer with access to supplies.

Hard sound in some notes
The causes are in the strings and bridge (see previous section) or in the hammers.

Strings which contact each other in their dead lengths or rub the screws of a pressure bar tend to have a poor tone, as do those whose coils on the tuning pins touch the wrestplank or frame. Some improvement may be obtained by interweaving the dead lengths with a strip of felt. There is often a 'wild' or 'rogue' string or group of strings close to a frame bar. Such strings are always inclined to sound out of tune. Little can be done save by toning (Chapter 5), though it should be checked that such strings have not been replaced by wire of too thick a gauge.

Hard, over-bright tone is produced by hammer felts which have lost their elasticity. Sometimes the felt is compressed or eaten away, in middle and upper hammers by wear, or more generally by moth. Occasionally a foreign body such as a wood-shaving or a piece of glue will be found embedded in the hammer head.

Extreme treble hammers may be capped with very soft leather or thin felt, though this will have to extend beyond one hammer else the tone will be irregular. Bass hammers can be filed with sandpaper to a reasonable shape, if not too far gone, and hardened again as necessary with a hot iron (see Chapter 5, 'Toning'). Extreme treble hammers can be hardened with varnish, but this produces an eccentric tone and it is better to try ironing and to reduce the thickness of hammer felt to the minimum.

These are repairs of convenience only and not without risk. There is really no substitute for new felt (see next section), with its tension, on the hammers. For individual hammers salvaged old felts may be usable or, preferably, new felt can be bent tightly round with impact adhesive and cramped. The best solution is certainly for tuner or technician to send the action away for recovering by machine. In all cases toning will be needed around the affected area.

The 'Old Joanna' sound

There is a characteristic sound of the neglected and much used piano, which I so describe. Its causes are many and not all can be dealt with unless the piano is completely restrung, refelted and restored. Even then, a sunken soundboard may be an underlying factor. Full restoration is often not commercially worthwhile. However, some of this work can be done by the amateur of limited experience if he has time (the largest element in the cost)

and the performance and value of the instrument in its present state are such that he has little to lose. It should also be borne in mind that the tonal production of pianos from the nineteenth century and even a little later was not what we have come to expect of even a cheap modern upright.

Restringing of the plain wire strings is beneficial and practicable (see above, 'Note not sounding—total'). The great majority of derelict pianos have never been restrung, whereas the useful life of a string is perhaps not much more than a generation. It is best to take samples of wire to a supplier or else to use micrometer readings, for strings are not always of current standard gauges and there is a risk of damage if wire is used which is too thick, quite apart from the impairment of tone. In any case, there is merit in roughly tuning ('chipping') a semitone flat and only after five or so tunings attempting gradually to pull the level up to standard pitch if that is required. Wound strings can be replaced if new are available, but they are expensive, and cleaning and twisting (see 'Notes rattle, whistle or ring' above) will produce improvement.

Great benefit to tone will also be given by refelting hammers, but it is essential, if complete felting is undertaken, to have the covering done by machine or at least, if you attempt it by hand, to use properly weighted and tapered hammer felt. Felt is sold by weight, but a supplier will provide a suitable sheet or, possibly, half sheet (which will do about four sets) if you quote maximum bass thickness; measure this at the uncompressed side (not the face) of the hammer. A strong, impact-type glue is simplest to use. Remove old staples and sand down old glue after cutting off previous felt. Newly hand-stuck felt needs to be lightly filed at the edges to give it a face just convex, since the tension turns it out concave and in this condition the head will strike unison strings at different moments. Ignoring this simple matter will lead to dissatisfaction no matter what other work is done and will make unisons difficult to tune. Top felts usually need ironing, and the middle range needs careful toning with the needles to even out overall tone. At the very top, felt of the correct thickness may not be able to be compressed sufficiently by hand, in which case it will need to be reduced with the sand-file to brighten the tone. Two or three sticks of wood stuck with medium and fine grade abrasive papers will do for files. Aluminium oxide paper is suitable.

Depending on the age and condition of the felts, recovering (which is fairly costly, and very time-consuming if done at home) may not be needed. It may be possible to dress the heads back to reasonable shape with sandpaper and then to work on them cautiously, trying out at every step, with needles and iron. When re-shaping, the object is to achieve a rounded face (seen from the side), the surface very slightly convex (seen from the top), and filing should be mainly on the shoulders (Fig. 25). As far as

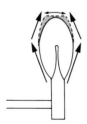

Fig. 25 Re-shaping a hammer, direction of filing

possible avoid the striking face, since otherwise tone will become dead and soggy and even ironing may not retrieve the situation. Work the sandfile from the back of the hammer towards the face,

brushing the latter only lightly to take out trenches and new fluff. If possible, file groups of hammers together rather than singly, so as to obtain a consistent profile.

The other major influences on tone which you may be able to adjust are the striking point and striking distance. Bringing the hammers up to 50mm from the strings is essential, and particularly necessary if the hammers have been dressed to shape. You can do it by moving the action further in, which will involve taking up lost motion at the key capstans; or by increasing the thickness of felt on the hammer rail, which will also affect the capstans; or by placing washers on the rail supports. Of course, if your hammers are refelted you may have to move the action back or lessen the felt at the hammer rail if the strike distance has previously been regulated. In grands, raise or lower the key capstans. Set the extreme top and bottom hammers by means of a ruler or gauge in the piano, then take the action out and set the rest by means of a strip of wood on pillars or a string between the pre-set hammers. In older, non-repetition grand actions, with the hammers resting on a rail, adjustment is as for uprights.

In uprights the strike distance tends to increase at the middle through bending of the hammer rail, thus spoiling the tone of the vital middle register. The best corrective is to remove the hammer rail and to straighten it with steam, or to replace it with straight timber. The alternative is to place a strip of felt on the rail beneath the most affected hammer shanks. Either way, regulation of the capstans is likely to be necessary afterwards.

The striking point has long been calculated to coincide as far as possible with the ninth harmonic, which is discordant—for example, with C it is the D three octaves higher. ('Harmonics' strictly include the fundamental pitch, wheres 'overtones' do not;

we could equally refer to the eighth overtone.) The principle followed is that if the string is struck near the node (the start of one of its vibrating partial sections) of the harmonic, the harmonic will be less audible. This means striking the middle and bass strings at about one eighth of their speaking length. Further up the piano an unmusical thump is produced if the string is struck this far down, and these strings tend to be struck as close to the upper bearing or pressure bar as can be arranged. There is not much scope for variation if the action is to be level and the top strings are to be struck sufficiently high, but tone can sometimes be improved by moving the action at the bass end, normally by screwing by a turn or two the cup in the bed on which the action rests. There is not normally cause to move a grand action in this way. If there are adjustable stops behind the action, they should be set so that the action is as close to the keyslip as possible without actually touching it and impairing movement by the soft pedal.

Piano will not play quietly

This sensation is connected with both touch and the state of the hammers. Many new pianos seem to lack a capacity for subtle playing because their actions are not run in and the resistances to touch are all rather emphatic. Thus the threshold, the least pressure required to move the hammer right to the string and cause escapement, is on the high side; if you try to play below it, you will get no sound at all, and your fingers seem to move towards a big kick from the escapement and an unexpectedly loud note.

The same effect is produced by maladjustment of the action (see the sections on 'Touch' above), so that the touch starts from a point so heavy that the fingers lack sensitive control, or the touch is very light until damper movement and escapement coincide,

when it is suddenly heavy. Such a piano, of course, requires regulation. A new piano will adjust itself within a few months, if regularly played, to a point where gradations of touch and volume stay the same for years.

Where the touch is acceptable, the trouble is likely to lie in the compacted felt of an older piano, which will require toning and possibly also dressing· (see Chapter 5 and above, 'The "Old Joanna" sound'). It will not come amiss to repeat here that the piano must be in tune before this work is attempted and that a slow and cautious approach is needed if more serious damage is not to be caused to the hammer felts.

Piano will not stay in tune

The common opinion of a piano which will not stay in tune is that the tuning pins are loose, and indeed this is very often the case in an elderly model. New pianos, however, receive many tunings in the factory and still may take time to settle down owing to the elasticity of their strings. This is even more true of older pianos restrung, where the elasticity of new wire may combine with loose pins. Whatever their age, pianos will not stay in tune if they are not tuned properly—if the tuner merely turns the pin and taps the key gently, the tension between dead and speaking lengths of string will even out when you play a martial piece and the strings will go flat. Older pianos may be badly affected by central heating (for which a moist pad or humidifier may help) and all pianos must be kept away from radiators, fires and the direct warmth of the sun. Finally, any piano is likely to need tuning after it has been moved.

A loose pin can be confirmed by marking it and the seating and noting that the marks drift apart. The only simple cure for loose pins is to drive them in further, provided that the wire does not touch the frame or wrestplank—to drive them further is in any case to risk cracking the plank. Slacken its string before driving in a pin. Suppliers stock liquid block restorer, which is applied to the pins, below the coiled wires, and swells the wood over a period of several days. An upright has to be turned onto its back for this treatment, and as far as possible the liquid should be kept from contact with the wires, which it will cause to rust (since it works by attracting and holding dampness). If the commercial product is not available, a mixture of methylated spirit and glycerine, with a little violin rosin flaked and dissolved in it, is quite effective. These restorers are most easily applied with a medicine dropper. Two or three drops to a pin usually suffice (though the treatment can be repeated) and it is necessary to make sure that they seep between pin and plank and do not merely lie on the surface of the plank. It is also possible to wedge pins with abrasive paper (such as aluminium oxide paper) or slips of veneer or rawlplug. In due course such treatment enlarges the holes and makes the situation worse. The ultimate solution is to have new pins of a larger size, if these are obtainable or, best of all, a new wrestplank.

Thus, one or two pins present a situation which may be retrieved for a while, but a piano with generally loose pins will, even if the wrestplank is undamaged, be troublesome and probably costly. At the worst, a new plank will have to be provided and accurately drilled, which is not a job for most amateurs to attempt.

Action noisy

Much noise in actions is located in the keys, caused principally by loose or worn bushings, slackness at the oval pin, and by felts on the keyframe which have disintegrated.

Faults in keys are rarely isolated—generally the best solution is to relay the keyboard. This is not difficult but it takes a great deal of time if commercial felt washers are not available. Replace the back felt to what is judged its original thickness, and the balance pin felts to a thickness at least sufficient to prevent the keys from knocking on the rail. This height must permit key fronts to dip 10mm, and to be horizontal when the front has been depressed to 5mm. Felts for the front rail oval pins are chosen or built up with this in view. The key fronts are precisely levelled by use of paper washers beneath the felts on the balance rail, and likewise key dip is limited by paper washers on the oval pins. If isolated keys strike the balance rail the sound will be much amplified when the keyframe is back in the strung piano, so any such keys must be sanded down. Where keys balance with fronts down, the procedure does not differ save that the keys must be laid balanced backwards, a strip of wood or suitable weight being placed on the backs. A home-made gauge for dip and a long straight-edge for levelling are useful—establish keys at either end so that the straight-edge can bridge the gap.

Uprights often suffer from the noise of rubbing bridle tapes and wires, and from the unmistakeable 'click' (immediately a key is released) of a jack landing on wood or glue instead of on the felt pad below the hammer butt. The bridle wires can of course be straightened. The penetrating 'click' can only be eliminated by teazing up the old felt with a needle or by putting in a new pad. This can sometimes be done by unfastening the bridle tape (having removed the key to allow the wippen to fall) and manipulating a new glued felt into position beneath the jack's tip. Alternatively and preferably, remove the action, unfasten the tape and take out the hammer to stick the felt to the butt.

Noises can be produced by loose checks and dampers. A check can be fixed by screwing it further into key or wippen, or, in a last resort, by resin glue. In grands, worn damper wire bushes lead to erratic noises and must be replaced completely or the enlarged holes brought back to size by insertion of slips of felt. A simple but elusive source of noise in grands is a loose wippen; ensure that the wippen flanges are firmly screwed up.

Small squeaks are usually caused by tight centres somewhere in the action. Centre pins are fixed into the part they secure, but their ends fit freely into the bushings on the flange (bracket). The 'whistling centre' can sometimes be cured by application of a hot soldering iron to the pin. A drop of water onto the wood surrounding the pin will do the trick eventually, but for a period will make the situation worse. For a radical cure, drive the pin out carefully with a punch and heat it or a wire of similar size, proceeding to slide the heated metal to and fro in the bushings. Hammer centres are often clamped into place by screwed metal slips rather than driven into the butts. The pins can then be moved easily, but they should be screwed tightly once repositioned or replaced. Pins must of course be cleaned of rust, with steel wool or a wire brush. Sometimes merely punching the pin in slightly from one side will provide quick improvement. What must be avoided is oiling the centre. Graphite is the only lubricant which may be used. Noise from the pedal action is dealt with below.

Other vibration

Unwanted vibration is tantalising. It may occur one day and be gone the next, it may occur only when a note of a certain pitch is played, or it may be more general. It may start only at the fullest fortissimo and develop subsequently at lower levels.

Establish first that the disturbance is within the piano. Vases, ornaments, glasses of clocks, keys and other small items may be set in vibration by a piano, often only at a certain pitch. Sometimes it is clear that the noise is in the instrument, but it may have to be established by eliminating other possibilities, taking trinkets from the room and observing the effect.

The site of vibration is adjacent masses, of which at least one is fairly free. Falls (lids) and music rests are prime offenders. The piano has to be played with such parts removed or rested on felt. In a good piano, surfaces either meet solidly, in which case they do not vibrate, or are damped by the use of felt and or rubber-headed nails, which can be obtained from hardware shops. (Always drill pilot holes for these nails to almost their full depth, or you will knock the heads off and may dent or crack the piano.) Often, regrettably even on new pianos, solid meeting surfaces are warped or are hinged crookedly so that they do not rest firmly on both sides.

In uprights the top lids and various catches securing the front panels merit attention, as does the back of the fall where it rests against front panel or sides when the instrument is open. A frequent area of trouble also is the bottom panel, which may vibrate against its latch or in its dowel holes below. On older pianos much use was made of recessed panels for ornament. These may be merely tacked into the main frames from behind and tend to come loose. The fault can be detected by pressing on the panels whilst the piano is played, and remedied by knocking the tacks in further or replacing them.

The grand has the disadvantage in a family that children can drop odds and ends into it, which fall onto the soundboard and may be invisible beneath the frame. A small vacuum cleaner, magnet, bent wire and any other accessories you can think of should be put to use. Otherwise, the principal sources are the front lid's folding back, the main lid's falling on the rim (which should be protected by felt or rubber), the lid prop (which should have felt or rubber to stop it contacting the frame), and the music rest, which must be well felted in its channels and rest in its supporting notches with weight on both sides. When the front lid is folded back with the key in the lock it is directly over the most vibrant part of the piano and, if there is trouble from this, little can be done except to remove or immobilise the key. It may in the long term be worth playing a good grand with the lid shut, the music rest lying on top with felt for protection, and only playing with the lid open for more special occasions. If the piano is always open it will accumulate a carpet of dust on the soundboard. This dust impairs tone and in time becomes hard to remove.

All screws should, of course, be firm, and this applies particularly to the small screws of a music rest or fall hinge which do not appear individually to take much strain and which, in a modern piano, may go into the edge of compressed wood fibre whose thread very rapidly strips. Larger screws, plugging with veneer or rawlplug or asbestos plugging compound, or simply gluing, are among the solutions. See also 'Pedal action noisy' below.

The pedals

Sustaining pedal stays on or does not work
The defect may be in the pedal mechanism or in the adjustment of dampers. The former is more likely if depressing the pedal has no effect, and the latter if only some strings seem to be affected. Observation of the dampers as the pedal is used will tell.

Pedal mechanisms themselves are virtually self-explanatory (see Figs. 9, 10, 10ª, 17). The commonest faults are with broken springs —evident from failure or partial failure of the pedal to rise—and short or missing connecting rods. The rods may not be properly located or they may leave far too much slack to be taken up. It is usual to adjust the pedals with about 8mm free play (see Chapter 4, 'The pedals').

When the pedal is used, uprights' dampers are operated by a metal rod underneath the damper tails. This is cranked and is turned by the pedal connecting rod so that it pushes the tails out and raises the dampers. Grands' dampers are raised by a rail beneath the levers, this being raised by a hinged tongue with which the connecting rod engages. The levers should lie level above the rail and if they do not do so the damping action with or without the pedal will be erratic. To retain this level setting, all but the most minor adjustment of the dampers to the keys should (once the level, giving some half of the key-dip's depression before the damper starts to move, has been found) be made at the keys rather than at the damper grubscrews.

Uprights' damper wires have to be bent against the strings until the dampers similarly rise in a straight line when the pedal is used, adjustment to action through the keys being made by bending the spoons. It may be necessary to increase or reduce felt on the damper tails where they are worn by the rod. Sometimes the tails are fitted with individual screws for taking up wear here. The tails should rest just on or free of the rod when the pedal is not in use; if they actually press on it, the dampers will be raised from the strings artificially and this will adversely affect consistent damping (see 'Staccato impossible or poor' above).

The necessary play in the action of the pedal should be obtained by the setting of the connecting rods and levers, not by allowing large slack between the rail and damper levers, or between the rod and damper tails.

Soft pedal has little effect

In the grand, the action will fail to shift sufficiently and failure is due to an obstruction at the right-hand end of it, to breakage of the angled piece which moves the keyframe, or to excessive slack in the connecting rod's adjustment. The stop in the right-hand key-block must be set so that the hammers cleanly strike two strings of a trichord when the pedal is depressed.

In the upright, by contrast, the setting of the soft pedal can be varied. If the hammer rail does not move far enough forward, slack must be taken up in the rod with felt, or in the lever with which it is attached to the pedal, unless of course the screw over the pedal can be sufficiently adjusted itself. It is common in older pianos for the cranked bracket on the hammer rail, which connects with the rod, to come loose and to introduce play. All that is needed is to fix it with larger screws or by plugging the holes.

If the pedal action is satisfactory and the upright's hammer rail reduces the strike distance by about half, the hammer felts must come under suspicion (see 'Piano will not play quietly' above).

Soft pedal causes keys to dip

This is peculiar to uprights. Since the half-blow system involves pushing the hammers forward on the hammer rail, it may also entail taking weight off the key-backs, according to the tightness of the tapes. If the tapes are such that the wippens are raised at all when the pedal is operated, and the keys naturally balance forwards, then of course the fronts of the keys will dip. If the keys balance backwards, they will move little, but the raising of the wippens will still excessively affect touch since there will be a gap before the capstans meet the wippens. Therefore tapes should be adjusted as far as possible to result in little or no movement of the wippens when the soft pedal is depressed. If this means very slack tapes when at rest, the soft pedal action may have to be lowered at the lever screw. If keys dip unevenly, this shows that the tapes need adjustment by bending the bridle wires.

Pedal action noisy

This is one of the commonest faults and is often tolerated unnecessarily, for cure is almost always possible though the best solution depends on experiment, for which the tuner himself simply has not time.

Uprights are most affected. Often the bottom boards were never strong enough, there is no central support, and in due course they come unglued owing to the strain of the pedal-work. The best answer is solid carpentry with the instrument on its back. The next weakness is the pivot blocks in which the pedal levers swing. These may be only glued or only screwed and come partly loose. Remove them, and both glue and screw them, taking particular care that they are properly in line with the lever when it is set up (for often they have been slightly crooked and so have taken unnecessary strain). The slots in these blocks and also the holes for the pins can be lined with felt. The pins should be a close but not a grinding fit. They can be lubricated with graphite grease or vaseline and graphite, and it may help if the pins are heated before being pushed in.

Many modern uprights use a bent leaf-spring as a pivot as well as for a spring. If this cracks, it can be replaced with the alternative block and pin with a coiled spring, which will be easier to obtain. Coiled springs should be sunk into holes on both lever and bottom board, and the holes should be lined with felt. The spring should be greased. These precautions are necessary because the path of the lever's end is eliptical rather than vertical and some friction is bound to occur. The pivot of the pedal itself will require similar greasing, and there should be a thick felt or soft leather washer beneath the nut on the pedal screw. The rubbing of this screw's head beneath the pedal is often troublesome—again, because its path is not in a straight line—and a leather washer is needed unless the bolt is fixed to the pedal. The top and bottom of where the pedal protrudes from the case should have a good cushion of felt and it must be ensured that there is ample clearance at the sides.

The same principles apply to grands, though it has to be borne in mind that their greater resonance leads to dull pedal sounds at the best of times. The springs are in the tongue beneath the body of the piano for the sustaining pedal and, of course, in the stout spring pressing against the treble end of the keyframe for the soft pedal.

Access to the grand's pedals is by unscrewing the whole lyre or support apparatus and removing the cover at the bottom (Fig. 26). Here the pedals will be found pivoted on pins passing into short dowels driven loosely up into the base. These pedals, of course, swing from the middle, not from the back as in uprights, since the change from depression to upward movement must be produced by the pedal rather than by levers.

This system does not normally give much trouble, though lubrication and replacement of worn leather washers are necessary and the dowels should be replaced or wedged to a close fit in the base block if they are loose (since otherwise the thrust is borne

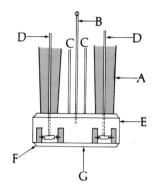

Fig. 26 Structure of grand pedal trapwork
A Support or lyre beam
B Rear supporting rod
C Ornamental and reinforcing rods
D Pedal operating rods
E Cut-out wooden block base
F Dowel in block, bearing the pedal pivot with washer
G Thin bottom cover

by the weak base cover). What does have to be watched is that the leather slabs at the ends of the pedals, on which the rods rest and press, are good and unworn. If the leather is hard and shiny it should be replaced, or a thin layer be shaved off its top. For soft pedal action, levelling the ground beneath the keyframe with fine sandpaper and steel wool and lubricating it with wax polish should remove any scraping sounds. The noise of the keyframe's reaching either side of the piano can be dealt with by adding felt to the stops. The shift action cannot be made entirely noiseless, but its sound should not be obtrusive when the piano is being played.

Further information

Dates of pianos

The following contain lists of piano numbers and dates arranged under manufacturers:

Pierce Piano Atlas (Bob Pierce, 2188 Lakewood Boulevard, Long Beach, California 90815).

H.K. Kerzog, *Piano-Nummern* (Verlag das Musikinstrument, 6 Frankfurt a.M., Klübestrasse 9).

Further Reading

(a) General and Historical★

Closson, E. *History of the Piano* (1944), tr. D. Amos, ed. R. Golding (1974)

Dolge, A. *Pianos and their Makers* (1911, reissued Dover, N.Y., 1972)

Ehrlich, C. *The Piano, a History* (1976)

Grover, D.S. *The Piano, Its Story from Zither to Grand* (1976)

Harding, R.E.M. *The Pianoforte, its History . . .* (Cambridge, 1933, 2nd ed., Gresham Books, 1978)

Harrison, S. *The Grand Piano* (1976)

Kentner, L. *Piano* (1976)

Sumner, W.L. *The Pianoforte* (1966)

Van Barthold, K. and Buckton, D. *The Story of the Piano* (1975)

★ Many of these works also contain material of practical interest.

(b) Practical

Fischer, J.C. *Piano Tuning, a Simple and Accurate Method for Amateurs* (1907, reprinted, N.Y., 1975)

Piano Tuning, Regulating and Repairing (Philadelphia, 1970)

Howe, A.H. *Scientific Piano Tuning and Servicing* (N.Y., 3rd ed., 1963)

Nalder, L.M. *The Modern Piano* (1927)

Stevens, F.A. *Piano Tuning, Repair and Rebuilding* (Chicago, 1972)

White, W.B. *Piano Tuning and Allied Arts* (Boston, Mass., 5th ed., 1946)

Theory and Practice of Piano Construction (1906, reprinted, N.Y., 1975)

Wolfenden, S. *A Treatise on the Art of Pianoforte Construction* (1927, reprinted 1975)

Other Sources

The following associations are primarily professional, but may be willing to assist with enquiries:

Institute of Musical Instrument Technology, 20, Disraeli Road, London, W.5.

Music Trades Association, 29, Exhibition Road, London, S.W.7.

Piano Advisory Service, 30, Eastbourne Terrace, London, W.2.

Piano Manufactuers' Association, 30, Eastbourne Terrace, London, W.2.

Piano Publicity Association, 30, Eastbourne Terrace, London, W.2.

Piano Trade Suppliers Association, 18a, Northampton Square, London, E.C.1.

Piano Tuners Association, 5, Northdown, Ashford, Kent.

Parts and Materials

Information as to suppliers of parts, tools and materials is given in:

Directory of Suppliers to Craftsmen Instrument Makers (1975), Scottish Development Agency (Small Business Division), Edinburgh, E.H.3 7H.Z., Scotland.

Profession of Piano Tuning and Technology

In the United Kingdom, entry to the career is by way of a 3–5 year apprenticeship with a factory or, occasionally, a retailer, possibly with day-release for acquiring a City and Guilds qualification. Full and part time courses are offered also by some Local Authorities, by the London College of Furniture (41–71, Commercial Road, London, E.1) and by other institutions. Special facilities exist for the blind and handicapped.

There is as yet no recognised licence or qualification for tuners and technicians. The nearest to such a thing is Membership of the Piano Tuners Association. The requirements for this are stringent, being basically two years' practical experience after completing a recognised course or apprenticeship or, in the absence of this, the passing of specific practical tests. The public can confidently place their pianos in the hands of Members, but good tuners are in demand and inevitably there are also proficient tuners who are not Members.

Discussions have for some time been in progress between such bodies as the Piano Manufacturers Association and Piano Tuners Association to regularise the situation, perhaps by a comprehensive system of licensing to practice, but it may be some years before there is any outcome in the shape of a recognised qualified profession. There is undoubtedly a need to protect the public in this area, and there is no reason at all why it should conflict with amateur interests in the subject.

Index

Index